A Memoir of No One in Particular

Also by Daniel Harris

Cute, Quaint, Hungry and Romantic: The Aesthetics of Consumerism

The Rise and Fall of Gay Culture

A Memoir of No One in Particular

Particular

*In Which Our Author Indulges
in Naïve Indiscretions,
a Self-Aggrandizing Solipsism,
and an Off-Putting Infatuation
with His Own Bodily Functions*

Daniel Harris

BASIC
BOOKS

A Member of the Perseus Books Group
New York

All doodles that appear in this book are by Daniel Harris and were drawn
on pads of adhesive notes.

Published by Basic Books,
A Member of the Perseus Books Group

Designed by Reginald Thompson
Set in 12-point Cochin by The Perseus Books Group

The Library of Congress has cataloged the hardcover edition as follows:
Harris, Daniel, 1957-
    A memoir of no one in particular / Daniel Harris.
        p. cm
    ISBN 0-465-02844-6
    1. Harris, Daniel, 1957- 2. Gay men—United States—Bibliography. I.
Title.

HQ75.8 .H37 A3 2002
305.38'9664—dc21
[B]
                                                            2001052536

paperback ISBN 0-465-02845-4

03 04 / 10 9 8 7 6 5 4 3 2

This book is dedicated to someone in particular.
And also to Joaquin Martinez-Pizarro and Amelia Arenas,
my best readers, my best friends.

Contents

1

Beginning

When I began to write this book, I viewed it as a satirical attack on the recent fashion for memoirs, for nostalgic, first-person reminiscences. Avoiding the personal point of view, I wanted to examine my behavior impersonally, to write the memoir of a nameless individual, the autobiography of both no one in particular and everyone in general. Rather than casting wistful glances back at my past and presenting a narrative account of my psychological development, I wanted to step out of my shoes and adopt the unsparingly objective stance of an observer in the monkey house, a bespectacled primatologist studying the curious antics of a creature in captivity scurrying around its cage. I would use myself as a pretext for probing the banalities of daily life, for rediscovering the unexplored territory of the commonplace and the habitual, for snooping around my messy desk and unmade bed, spying into what I keep in my junk drawers and beneath my kitchen sink, and staking out the shady goings-on in my bathroom and clothes hamper. I did not want to write a nonfiction novel, a docdramatic re-creation of my unhappy childhood, troubled relations with my parents and two sisters, failed love affairs, battle against depression, midlife crisis, brush with alcoholism, but rather a type of anthropological *bildungsroman* that would tell the story of how I occupy a specific set of rooms, how I interact with the things I possess, how I cook and bathe, laugh and make faces. Mine would be a memoir without time, an account of a man without a past, a perverse behavioral experiment that concentrated only on those aspects of daily living we all share, on how we groom ourselves, wash our clothes, cheat, make love, laugh, lie.

But as I began to write, I found myself asking if it wasn't a little disingenuous of me to pretend that I was "no one in particular," if my experience of life was as universal as it should be for such a project, and if a statistical sampling of one — and a somewhat idiosyncratic statistic at that — was sufficient to draw credible conclusions about our most mundane behaviors. It became increasingly apparent that I was an unlikely guinea pig for my anthropological study, that the way I live only occasionally reflects the way the majority of people live, that an effete homosexual who spends six days of the week reading and writing, who lounges around for most of his waking hours in his house robe and pajamas, and who ekes out a sub- sistence living working one long shift as a word processor, scraping by in America's most expensive city, may not, in the final analysis, be an ideal candidate for the starring role of Everyman.

My conception of what I originally characterized as an "anti-memoir" thus began to change in order to accommodate my specimen's shortcomings and eccen- tricities. I decided that I would incorporate more per- sonal commentary than I intended, that I would indeed present a schematic chronology of how I developed, but that I would do so only secondhand by recounting the history, not of myself, but of an inanimate object or activity pivotal to my life, as I do in my two most con- ventionally autobiographical chapters, "Writing" and "Reading." Instead of starting at birth and ending at the age of forty-three, I would examine how my wardrobe and sex life have evolved, how my relationship to books has changed, how I cannot lie with the same poetic license that made my childhood fibs so colorful nor write with the same degree of hysterical animation. In this way, by telling my life story vicariously through things rather than events, through prose and facial expressions, underwear and book bags, idioms and in- jokes, I would at once retain the high level of objectivity I sought as an antidote to the traditional memoir and yet avoid presenting myself as something I very obviously am not, an ordinary Joe Blow with a family, mortgage, and nine-to-five job, a type of man who would never even think of undertaking the sort of self-dissection I set out to perform armed with a computer, some tape cassettes, and an appalling lack of shame — for that matter, of taste.

Something deeply personal lies behind this cinéma vérité experiment. The thick armor of vanity that protects my ego from the knowledge of its own insignificance has at last been pierced by the dawning realization that my literary ambitions may remain unfulfilled and that I will probably never secure the audience I once believed I would reach. Perhaps even here I am simply making a case for myself, expressing resentment, railing against the injustice of neglect, begging for my fifteen minutes of fame. But if there is a chip on my shoulder, I must remove it. Having waited nearly twenty years for that most fickle of Godots, a readership, I find myself at a typical midlife crossroads in which I am beginning to look for happiness outside the frustrating business of "making it," an enterprise that has consumed so much of my time and attention, leading me to neglect my enjoyment of the world for a hypothetical future. By reducing myself to nothing more than a kind of living camcorder, an intellectual device for exposing the method and meaning of the prosaic, I undertake a search-and-rescue mission to recover what remains of my life after I have stripped it of all illusions of wealth, fame, and glamour, refusing to live in a constant state of deferred gratification. My efforts to reengage with what I call my material unconscious, with what I eat and how I clean my apartment, can be understood as a Cartesian quest for absolutes, for truths that rest on foundations more secure than my aspirations. In the course of this experiment, I transform myself into the Robinson Crusoe of the quotidian, a shipwrecked castaway who must relearn life at its most basic physical level, explore its fundamental premises, teach himself all over again how to talk, dress, write, read, and bathe.

Such a thorough undertaking requires strong measures. My most incriminating observations rest on a truism that has governed much of my adult life: that articulating a secret robs it of its power over us, that the unutterable cannot withstand its utterance. Much of the behavior I discuss is a source of acute embarrassment for people, who cannot bring themselves to admit that they examine the tissues on which they blow their noses, lie constantly, and adore being dominated in bed, even though feminism has taught them that the pleasure of submission is, on ideological grounds, inadmissible. My tendency to hack my way through the thicket of taboos that has grown up around a culture naively convinced of its permissiveness rests on my heartfelt conviction that silencing fears only intensifies them, that the hygienic rite of confession makes one strong, and that the rattle of skeletons in one's closet provides the softest and most soothing of lullabies.

The memoir continues to enjoy enormous popularity among readers because we are a prurient culture and enjoy watching people bare their souls, confessing their adulterous affairs, attempted suicides, incarcerations in asylums, incestuous relationships with their fathers, and reconciliations with long-lost illegitimate children. There is nothing that can shock us when it comes to the secrets of the heart, but this is not the case when it comes to the secrets of the body, to the positions we prefer during sex, to our hygiene, to the nasty habits we engage in behind closed doors, what we sniff and where we scratch, subjects about which the less said, the better, which are none of your business and, what's more, too trivial for serious discussion. We pride ourselves on being unflappable, on having seen and heard and even done almost everything there is to see and hear and do, and yet we rarely discuss with others the messy biological realities of our lives, which we conceal behind a veil of discretion and taste.

Some will undoubtedly find my book too detached, and still others, because I look so closely at my habits, self-indulgent and narcissistic. I am at once impersonal and too personal, treating myself as a specimen in an experiment and yet forcing the reader to get too close for comfort to the minutiae of my life.

I grew up in a liberal, middle-class family. My father was a disaffected Jew who, much to his mother's anguish, married a disaffected Southern Baptist, a country girl who found God in a revival tent in rural Missouri after she mistakenly raised her hand when the preacher began roaming the audience in search of sinners who had not been saved. She lost God only a few minutes later when she exited the tent, and so my sisters and I were spared any religious education whatsoever — a great blessing, in my view, even though my father regrets our lack of faith now that he is retired and, like so many aging Jews, is prone to waxing sentimental about the idols of the tribe. He was first the dean of a university in Wisconsin (on a hunch, he left his job in the late 1960s only to see his successor burned in effigy the following year during campus riots) and later became a therapist who lived modestly so that his low-income clients could afford his fees, which they often paid with the barter of their handicrafts — paintings on pieces of driftwood, lopsided clay pots, and macramé plant hangers. My mother was the director of a large day care center located in a crime-ridden, drug-infested housing project in the heart of Appalachia. Here, as a volunteer, I attempted to give the children the physical affection that many of them were not receiving at home, kissing every sore thumb, scraped knee, and snotty nose within a ten-mile radius. My parents were outspokenly antimaterialistic and lived more frugally than they needed, perhaps out of respect for their own humble beginnings—a lesson that has served me well ever since, given that, after leaving graduate school in 1985, I have refused to work more than two days a week as a word processor. Politically, they were both left of center, and they instilled in me strong democratic principles, discouraging me from viewing myself as superior to others and welcoming my eclectic set of friends, often drawn from the dregs of humanity: a wall-eyed Seventh Day Adventist; a fourteen-year-old black unwed mother; and, much later in life, an alcoholic prostitute and daughter of a Mafioso.

My parents' belief in the importance of social service organizations, along with the radicalism of the counter-culture (by the age of thirteen, I was a gangly hippy with a huge Afro of frizzy split ends), fostered in me a fiercely egalitarian commitment to helping the poor and fighting for minority rights. My politics, however, simply did not jibe with an aspect of my life that pulled me in exactly the opposite direction: my homosexuality. I grew up taunted by the very people I now hoped to serve, the sons of Wisconsin farmers, gang members in Buffalo, and red-necks in Appalachia, bigots whose scorn I met halfway with my own contempt, a self-protective superciliousness I cultivated by embracing the very things my peers despised, most notably, literature and art. I became a snob, an elitist, a dandy who, during one mercifully brief period in early adolescence, adopted a cane and, during a much longer period — in fact, for the rest of my life — a faint British accent.

But at the same time that I was looking down my nose at the unwashed masses, I was kissing their children, malnourished six-year-olds who came to the day care center starving, with black eyes, distended bellies, and rotten teeth. Early in my adolescence, I was torn between the political lessons of equality that were a key part of my moral education and my survival tactics as an effeminate teenager — my use of books, culture, and an air of sophistication to project the kind of power my heterosexual schoolmates found on the basketball court and the football field.

As an adult I experienced this tension in another way. After five years in graduate school, I fell through the cracks into a cultural limbo, the ill-defined realm of the "independent scholar," that elephant's graveyard of Ph.D. dropouts who, the victims of either the tenure crisis or the civil wars decimating humanities departments, found work as temps and taxi drivers, waiters and word processors. I became an autonomous intellectual in the age of the academization of *belles lettres*, a decision that has consigned me to the Gulag of the intelligentsia, an isolation in which I keenly experience the lack of literary companionship. My disenchantment with the university has only intensified my alienation from my culture, which is rooted both in my sexuality and in the fact that I have no institutional affiliation whatsoever and have been forced to pursue the life of the mind under nearly monastic conditions.

The tension between my elitism and my liberalism, my at best marginal standing as a freelance writer for literary quarterlies, and my desire to be part of a larger community, appears in the unlikeliest places. It works itself out in my wardrobe, sense of humor, voice, and prose style. In fact, it underlies the very structure of this book, which often becomes a dialogue between the separatist and the democrat, the memoirist and the social scientist, the biographer who thinks of himself as a unique individual with a highly personal view of the world and the zoologist who looks at himself purely as a specimen. In respect to many of the fears, desires, and routines I discuss, I could easily be describing not an East Coast intellectual but a truck driver from Peoria; both read in the bathroom, leave the cap off the toothpaste, refuse to discard broken answering machines, suffer from catastrophic name blocks, smell their own farts, launder their sheets less often than they should, and pick their scabs.

It is unlikely, however, that the truck driver from Peoria suffers from my own morbid fear of botulism, buys his gym trunks from the women's section of sporting goods stores, or worries about the unsightly gray hairs spreading over his shoulder blades and sprouting out of his nostrils and earlobes. The point of view of my book thus oscillates between the specific and the general, between my life story as told through inanimate objects and a careful analysis of behaviors characteristic of the species as a whole. In this democratic exercise in self-demolition, this act of public suicide, I reduce myself to the lowest common denominator and attempt to reestablish my connection with others. It is difficult, after all, to harbor any illusions of your grandeur when you admit to thousands of readers that you are a nose-picking, toenail-biting sufferer of gas attacks who, in your youth, wrote — worse, preserved — reams of egregious nature poems.

In many respects, I am the perfect consumerist human being: I have stuck myself together like Mr. Potato Head from traits I purchased in stores and pulled off book shelves. I have divorced myself from my family and my past and reinvented who I am, what I look like, how I act, eat, talk, dress, gesture, and even decorate my apartment. I am a typically modern, deracinated person with no moorings in history, religion, community, class, clan, nor even the corporation, the major institution from which people now derive their sense of purpose. I have turned my back on every single presupposition that once lent structure to our lives: I have no religion; grew up in an entirely secular household devoid of rituals; feel deeply alienated from the materialism and conventionality of my minority group, the so-called gay "community"; am revolted by the pervasive postmodernism of the university; and, although I have a steady job, now work only one twelve-hour shift on Sundays, scarcely enough time to provide me with a very strong feeling of mission.

My interest in uncovering the secret life of my material unconscious, of the habitual and the pedestrian, is not only part of my campaign to take myself down a notch. In the early 1980s, I became a book reviewer. I pursued this line of work until the late 1980s, when assignments slowly began to dry up, partly because my venomous tone made me unappealing to all but the hardiest breed of newspaper editors and partly because I was so bad, my prose style so undeveloped. If I was to continue writing, which by then was essential to my mental health, I needed a subject to replace the galleys I was no longer receiving, and since very little happens in the life of an intellectual, which is largely a matter of internal reactions to ideas, I turned to the objects I saw around me—on my desk, in my drawers, beneath my bed, all of which I "read" and "reviewed" exactly as I had once "read" and "reviewed" books. It was only a small step for me to transfer the techniques of New Critical close analysis, which were part of my graduate training in literature, to the labels on my deodorant, the treads on my sneakers, the garbage at the bottom of my book bag, and the obsessive doodles I so immodestly frame and place on my walls. The myopic approach I take to the debris of my life is the occupational deformity of a literary critic, the perpetual squint of the scholar accustomed to examining the microscopic details of texts—diction and metaphors, syntax and punctuation. I have substituted myself for the missing book and am, in a very real sense, now reading my life. With this in mind, I begin my first lesson in self-literacy, a conventional *explication de texte*, which will be followed by a close reading of, among other more figurative "texts," my closet, bathroom, and voice.

2

Writing

To Philip Shehadi (1957–1991)
who rescued me from the diaries

I am eight years old and I am writing to my homesick sister Lynn, who is spending the summer at Camp Far Horizons, languishing over weenie roasts and moping through campfire sing-alongs. She has been badgering my parents to force me to send her a letter, which, in my callous disregard of what I view as pure sentimentality, I write only under the direst threats of being grounded or having my twenty-five-cent allowance revoked. It is the sole letter that remains from my childhood and thus ground zero of my prose style, the nucleus from which everything I have written since has emerged:

Dear Lynn,

I am having fun. Hammy got out today. This is one of the thing that happened to. Mary Margret

>couldent find her aracecer she looked and looked I
>look in my desk and there it was. Last night there
>was a fire we saw the fire. I miss you two.
>
>Love Dan.

Just as the trauma of potty training is said to linger on
in the unconscious, where it continues to exert an oblique
and subliminal influence on our daily lives, so my formative rhetorical experiences still lie at the foundation of
what were eventually to become my distinguishing mannerisms as a writer. Beneath the chaos of this dyslexic
note, one can see, if not the seeds of my later prose style,
then at least a characteristic attitude towards the act of
writing—specifically, a snide disesteem for what was to be
my very first audience, my woebegone sister roughing it
in the wilds of rural Illinois, sleeping under mosquito nets
and peeing in port-o-potties. Even here in this imbecilic
paragraph, whose jagged letters lean crazily in various
directions, steering a drunken course above and below the
paper's ruled lines, it is possible to discern a hint of irony,
a distasteful sense of the perfunctory nature of a task I
undertook only after being blackmailed by my parents.
The feeble litany of "the thing that happened to"—the
madcap chase after our fugitive guinea pig or the gripping
saga of the purloined "aracecer," both guaranteed to make
Lynn's eyes brim with tears—is suffused with the boredom of my begrudging compliance with my parents' ulti-
matums.

Here I am eight years later, now sixteen, again writing to an older but no less homesick Lynn, who this time is pining away during her first weeks at college, as usual full of recriminations about my inconsiderate silence, by now a shortcoming with which she is all too familiar. Whereas the irony in the preceding letter was implicit in my barely concealed reluctance to do my brotherly duties, it is now explicit, having hardened into the priggish stance of a sarcastic old man who can scarcely bring himself to put pen to paper, so bothersome, so beneath his dignity, does he find the routine of carrying on small talk with his sister:

Dear Lynn,

I was horribly torn to see you leave us Sunday. I just realized that my little child had matured and was ready to accept the responsibilities of an adult.

I really have nothing to tell you and am tempted to end my letter presently. However, that would be rude. Letters are so farcical!

Anyway I love you and hope your classes are going to your satisfaction. Have you learned Newton's laws yet? I certainly hope so. (God, I hate writing letters.)

Today was a nice day. It was an enjoyable day. It was a good day. How was your day?

Shit, Lynn, I can't write anymore.
SO I WROTE YOU! SO THERE!!

Love,
Dan

I open the letter by infantilizing my reader and then by insulting her, putting her in her place with such patrician circumlocutions as "presently" and "to your satisfaction," words that show how "farcical" a genius like myself finds this family charade of keeping in touch, which I burlesque so effectively in the repetition of "today was a nice day." As insignificant as this letter is, its mock solemnity and phony periphrasis reflect one of the major assumptions I made about prose during this seminal period in my literary education, an assumption that was to transform my letters from chatty, intimate exchanges into nothing less than aggravated assaults against my unsuspecting and entirely innocent readers. From the time I took my first faltering steps as a writer, my whole concept of style was inextricably linked in my mind with an act of condescension, of *noblesse oblige*, of distancing myself from an audience I believed was inferior to me. Style became a form of rebellion, a way of defining myself against my immediate environment, of exaggerating my superiority to it, of sealing myself off from its banality and lack of sophistication. Even at the age of sixteen, I had learned to exploit prose as a means of self-construction, of fabricating a false identity (with a wig and a Groucho Marx nose), a disguise I used to protect the painfully fragile and unformed personality of an insecure and effeminate young homosexual stranded, as I saw myself, in a small, homophobic Southern town. Using the limited resources available in my rhetorical arsenal (in particular, this unbearably affected pretense of irony), I created a "voice" dripping with the sarcasm of a snickering, prematurely aged aesthete.

But although my foremost concern in these early letters was to convey the impression of scorn, rejecting a more colloquial style for one strewn with what I perceived as dignified euphemisms, the prose of this period is not as arrogant as most readers probably find it but has already begun to exhibit the symptoms of a rhetorical affliction that persists up until the present. On the one hand, at the age of seventeen, I am so smug that I write home to my parents during my first weeks at Oberlin College in the stiff, ceremonial manner of Wodehouse's Jeeves. In a florid style appropriate to another century, I make weighty proclamations about such things as the fact that school "does not inspire a convivial mood for me"; that the campus's Gay Union is "horribly disorganized but most beneficial"; that "I do not relish the contrived get-togethers" of freshman orientation; and that "I have been troubled of late because I find that I must constantly fight the unending battle of dealing with the progeny of America's most prominent and most tiring people, the indolent rich." But although I write in the quaintly anachronistic style of the beleaguered heroine of a nineteenth-century epistolary novel, I am obsessed with the pretentiousness of others, whose haughty "airs" I am constantly ridiculing, even as I am oblivious to my own grandiloquence. At the same time that I attempt to express the world-weary fatigue of someone far more disillusioned than I could legitimately claim to be at the age of seventeen, I tend to displace my affectations onto my fellow students, as when I observe that "the conservatory, or excuse me, THE CONSERVATORY, is just as pretentious as it sounds" or when I state that, while resigned to my lonely lot as a courageous nonconformist, I nonetheless feel marooned in "a sterile world of intelligent, pretentious, and frankly boring adolescents."

The divided state of mind implicit in this disingenuous preoccupation with the pomposity of others often led me to subvert my grave, unctuous manner by lowering my style as drastically as I elevated it in my efforts to belittle and intimidate my audience. No sooner do I screw in the monocle with which I constantly seem to be scrutinizing my peers, than it pops out, as I temporarily abandon the pose of the prudish spinster for that of a bawdy, foulmouthed brat who takes particular delight in shrieking obscenities from the sidelines. My style lurches from the Latinate to the colloquial, from the sublime to the ridiculous, as when I tell my sisters that Oberlin's ostentatious library, a technicolor extravaganza that I describe as "enigmatic, intriguing, and marvelous," "makes [our hometown library] look like a toilet, girls," or when I praise a pianist friend whose technique is, to say the least, refreshingly unsophisticated: "after a stormy piece of Beethoven, he burped; after a delicious piece of Chopin, he delivered an impassioned fart." This ghastly oxymoron ushers the reader into the very heart of an adolescent persona that attempts to be two entirely contradictory things at once, both exquisite and ribald, aesthetic and raunchy.

The deflationary tendency of my style emerged out of an identity that was fluid and unstable, shifting between extremes, now starchy and hifalutin, now racy and vulgar. A profound undercurrent of self-loathing, a panicked longing to rip off the demure, grim-visaged mask that was suffocating my style, makes my complacent manner as strident and unnatural as a falsetto. Resorting to vulgarity as an antidote to my own piss-elegance, I was clearly disgusted by my pretentiousness, even as I was unable to admit it to myself. I therefore took refuge in a protective self-ignorance by mocking the foibles of others and by infusing my stateliness with deliberate bathos.

This Janus-faced creature, who tries to be at once Jane Eyre and Moll Flanders, soon turned to another kind of writing altogether, the second in a long succession of masks that I have adopted and, soon after, discarded in the interminable process of inventing (and reinventing) my prose style. After a series of encounters with various charismatic extremists, with whom I inevitably fell in love and therefore dotingly imitated, the facetiousness of my early letters to my family mellowed into the deadly earnestness of the diaries I kept between the ages of seventeen and twenty. Dashed off in a kind of glandular frenzy, this astonishing document is a pastiche of both the precepts of my mentors and those of established authors whose incantatory styles dovetailed disastrously with my own intellectual immaturity. In these brooding reveries I combine the asceticism of St. Augustine's *Confessions*, the irrationality of Kierkegaard, the austerity of Thoreau, the delirium of the Transcendentalists, the nature worship of *The Prelude*, the preciosity of classical Chinese poetry, and the wisdom of Taoist philosophers. Here is a typical entry in its entirety:

> September 10, 1975
>
> The winds have blown all day long but they have not blown their madness away. Listening to the winds, I feel that they are working something out amongst themselves, something mad and profound, some protest from the heart of things. It rained several times while I was walking about, and each time I turned my face to the wind and closed my eyes so that the rain would wash me, open wound that I was this afternoon. To feel the peace of rain upon one's face, it makes one feel so changed. It is like the moon—it gives one hope. I wish the clouds would go away so that I could see the moon again.
>
> I am sad as dusk is sad, dusk that reaches my soul like a sigh of the day that is passing away into night. I am sad as the cool air of dusk or the clear blue of the shadows in dusk's dim light. I am passing like the light is passing or the wind is passing as it bends the tall weeds in a field. To the world I would say, from my heart I should speak, young boy that I am at heart, take me, world, into the world as one would lead a child by hand. I must touch the world as a branch softly stirred by the wind that brushes the air by its side. I am sitting by the window writing words that hold my sadness in

their hands, that touch me like a breeze. I am thinking of the kiss I gave my mother and the kiss that she returned, and both were soft as a petal that fell from its flower to my hand, soft as a blade of grass and both so lonely.

There will come a time when one's soul unfolds like cloth, and one will be amazed how it unfolds and unfolds. I wish that I would begin to unfold deep within me, to unfold like cloth, to hear the folds rustle like whispers, and to feel the peace of disclosing one's soul to the silence that unfolds. My God, how will I ever find my freedom? How will I ever break through the layer after layer of dead self that traps me in this cancerous hole of mine?

Gone is the ironic detachment of the cynic and in its place are the rapturous effusions of a raving nun in a trance, a tortured anchoress in her cell communing with the infinite. The exaggerated style of this introverted crank is uniquely expressive of the experience of adolescence. Comprising some 500 to 600 pages of dense prose poems written in biblical cadences, the notebooks give us direct access to the mind of an irrepressibly verbose poseur in the throes of a phase in personality development that is seldom documented, the psychologically complex process of teenage self-invention.

Given that the whole purpose of the diaries is to provide incontrovertible evidence of how sensitive I am, how responsive to "the sublime nobility of life, which moves to

such profound music," they are surprisingly unsensuous
and abstract, the observations of a refined shut-in writing
in a cork-lined room. Not only are the diaries totally non-
narrative, devoid of information about my daily life, but
they are free of concrete details about nature, their primary subject, which I am constantly describing, even though
I evoke a physical world that tends to evaporate into
clichés about lowering skies and mournful weeping willows, about "clouds in whose shifting light one overhears
the moon speaking to itself" and "early mornings that play
songs on my sad soul." If the oxymoron "impassioned fart"
is the figure of speech that best captures the tensions
wrenching apart my earliest prose style, the pathetic fallacy is the poetic convention that best expresses the self-
absorption with which I reel around a murky, romantic
landscape striking the poses of a wild-eyed poet. The following passage describes a walk I took around a lake at
Oberlin:

> I saw the water ripple on the lake and the clouds
> breaking above rebuking my smallness with their
> grandeur. The water spoke a silent language of sup-
> plication. A willow hung its head above the water
> that spoke, but it was either indifferent or resigned
> or deaf, for it responded to not a word, and the
> water continued its supplication.

This is an interior landscape, not an objective one, an
allegory, rather than a description of a real scene. It is I
who do the supplicating, not the rippling water, and it is

the harsh, cold world of "intelligent, pretentious, and frankly boring adolescents" that ignores my bleating cries for companionship, not the weeping willow, which, along with the clouds and the water, have simply become extensions of my poetic alter ego. Blinded by my emotions, which have transformed the objective world into a private amphitheater, I have allowed the pathetic fallacy to wipe out the landscape, imprisoning me in pure abstractions cut off from nature, the very entity from which I pretend to draw such nourishment.

As fundamental to the style of my journals as my tendency towards barren generalities is my understanding of the basic assumption on which the whole genre of the diary is presumably based: that it is written in a state of intense solitude. Far from being a jealously guarded act of self-communion, each entry in my notebooks is an elocutionary event that conveys the impression that it is being acted out rather than simply written down, an effect heightened by the way in which, like Hamlet, I tend to salute unseen participants ("Alex, my friend, let's get drunk and read poetry!") or address celestial bodies like the moon ("your pure crescent casts upon my tired eyes a peace that leaves me breathless with your age and wisdom"). Such histrionic features give my journals the old-fashioned tone of a nineteenth-century poetic recitation, as if I were an orator performing "Ozymandias," complete with a well-rehearsed dumb show of facial expressions and hand gestures. My prose becomes an occasion for the display of the skills with which I bully and rebut fictional opponents with vehement affirmations and indignant denials, with such statements as "No, I am wary of the established!" and "Yes, I will go [for a walk]!," just as I pose and answer my own rhetorical questions, plaintively querying, "How can I say to myself that I am weary of this empty life?" and "How does one harness one's changes so that one arrives at permanence?" Although it is central to the theater of my notebooks that the reader suspend disbelief and pretend that he is eavesdropping on an act taking place under conditions of complete isolation, it is obvious that I am convening an open house, a salon in which a vast assembly of admirers is huddling around my desk, listening in admiration as I whirl about the spotlight clutching my brow. The declamatory mode of this most rhetorical episode in my literary development is the result of a fundamental shift in the audience I am addressing, from the very real audience of a family of four unglamorous individuals, whom I treat so unjustly, to the imaginary audience of posterity, over which I fawn and toady, groveling at its feet in order to ingratiate myself well in advance of its arrival.

Although my diaries may appear to be outbursts of uncontrollable emotions ignited by raging adolescent hormones, they are in fact complex literary acts in which I am engaging in an entirely disingenuous sort of writing: the creation of an apocryphal biography of the artist as a young man. These are not journals in any ordinary sense of the word but memoirs incognito in which I stage-manage my own image, already thinking ahead, at the tender age of seventeen, to the sort of evidence a budding celebrity would need to amass in order to prove his embryonic greatness to his unborn fans. My notebooks therefore function as a time capsule that I left behind to be unearthed by my disciples, who were meant to study them as a form of advance PR for my illustrious future career. They are the ghostwritten confessions of a shameless perjurer who, although writing in the present, is actually inventing a literary past by plagiarizing the biographies of other poets and writers, all the while serving as his own Boswell, his own Eckermann, a live-in scribe dutifully taking down the dictation of an imaginary master. If there is anything at all authentic about this hoax, this precocious act of self-falsification in which I recreate myself in the image of Byron or the young Werther, it lies in the fact that its artificiality is in itself a measure of real unhappiness. Only someone profoundly disappointed with the tedium of his real biography would go to such extravagant lengths to counterfeit this separate, parallel existence, an invisible twin in whom I lived out my thwarted fantasies, much as housewives escape from the drudgery of cooking and cleaning by fleeing into Harlequin romances.

The lack of even the sketchiest outlines of a real scene in my diaries becomes a gauge of how fictional this world is, how far removed from everyday reality which would have supplied the concrete detail that I supplanted with generalities (when my sister Lee tells me that she is contemplating suicide, for instance, I offer her words of wisdom guaranteed to drive her straight to the medicine cabinet: "I said what comes from my heart, that every man is faced with the choice of idling away his hours on earth or raising himself up to embrace the sublime and that she must abandon even the remotest possibility of killing herself, for the gestation period of one's life will begin only when one has renounced forever an act that will confine one's spirit for all time to the grim infertility of a half-birth"). The inauthenticity of the diaries, in other words, is not just the outcome of lack of talent but of the basic vacuity of identity that lies at their core, the absence of a point of view, an emptiness that I attempted to fill by fabricating a personality from the raw materials of my reading. Despite their pretentiousness, the diaries offer a textbook example of the way in which an adolescent with literary ambitions initiates the process of self-construction. In them, I "found" myself, not by being faithful to my true nature, to some sort of fixed, permanent identity that we are erroneously supposed to have been born with, but by tearing frantically through a whole wardrobe of disguises. To find my own "voice," I appropriated the voices of others, piecing together a makeshift identity by performing ventriloquistic acts of homage to literary figures whose styles I parroted and, inevitably, perverted.

At the age of twenty, an abrupt change occurs and the diaries suddenly stopped, not because this dizzying juggernaut inexplicably ground to a halt, losing its momentum as I matured, but because I systematically destroyed the notebooks I had not previously entrusted to that most faithful and indiscriminate of archivists, my mother. Only four entries (written between the ages of twenty and twenty-two, and slipped between the pages of class notes that I took while attending Harvard Summer School) escaped the pyre, the sole remaining firsthand accounts of one of the most influential events of my life, my disastrous and pathetically unrequited obsession with my best friend, Philip. Although the entries comprise only ten pages smeared with erasures and crossed-out words, they show that an enormous leap in sensibility has occurred and thus provide the missing link between the wistful reveries I wrote before I met Philip in 1977 and the blisteringly satirical prose I wrote afterwards. Demoralized by this infatuation, I am no longer the arrogant impostor of the early notebooks but an insecure and compulsively self-deprecating person who, in reference to this degrading impasse, derides himself as "a goose, a fat thirteen-year-old girl with buckteeth and pimples and in love," "a faggot" who "thinks like a child" and wastes his time writing about "stupid matters like this goddamn obsession." The style of the early diaries and that of these four late entries are so antithetical, the one so smarmy, the other so snide, that it would be impossible to identify them as the prose styles of a single individual if one had no knowledge of the psychological upheaval that had intervened between them.

Though these late entries are not nearly as ironic as the decimating pans I was to write when I began reviewing books several years later, I am already skeptical about the sincerity of the early journals, which I dismiss as the sentimental meditations of a schoolboy. I now seem to be writing out of a genuine spirit of misery caused by an experience that has fundamentally altered the sense of complacency that made the early notebooks possible in the first place:

> I am embarrassed when I think of what it means to write diaries. It seems hilarious and absurd to me to write what one already knows, and so earnestly —as if one was revealing the events of the day to oneself for the first time. I think that the compulsion to diary-write comes from an inner store of melodrama . . . One projects an imaginary reader, a whole audience of important people, before which one sings one's song in the loveliest most demure cocktail dress, filled with passion, the center of attention at last — diary-writing is a closet case of the drag queen's dream.

The irony of the early letters has emerged again, but whereas before it arose as a means of defining myself against an audience whose insipidity I exploited as the rhetorical backdrop for my own genius, it has now reemerged as an indication, not of my readers' insignificance, but of my own — the result of my utter loss of self-esteem in the face of Philip's indifference. The weapon that I sharpened on my family I now turn back on myself, slashing into my self-congratulating presumptuousness as I characterize my past performances strutting before the footlights, spouting sagacious nonsense, as the antics of a drag queen silently wailing a lip-synched anthem of self-pity. My experience with Philip has been so shattering to my vanity as a rising literary superstar that it has penetrated the carapace of poetic clichés in which I had sealed myself, sheering away the entire mass of nauseous metaphors. Having lost this vainglorious sense of self-importance, I whirl around on myself like a viper and lunge at the now useless persona of the sibyl, the crazed prophetess whose hyperventilating theatrics are gradually disappearing as I crawl humiliated out of the wreckage of this relationship and adopt my third major mask, that of the cackling cynic, the disbeliever, an incorrigible doubting Thomas who has jettisoned forever the sanctimoniousness of his youth.

By the time I began reviewing books for small gay newspapers some three years later, my new persona had already hardened into what was to become the foundation of my "mature style." If the rhetoric of the diaries was intended to demonstrate my sensitivity, the rhetoric of my early reviews was intended to do just the opposite, to demonstrate my *insensitivity*, my toughness, my callousness as an unflappable critic who immobilized his prey like Medusa, freezing the authors he reviewed with the icy stare of the dispassionate professional. In the opening paragraphs of an essay on two gay novels, the reader looks in vain for even a trace of the soft-spoken figure who once claimed he could hear ponds muttering supplications to despondent weeping willows:

> Two recent releases by Houghton Mifflin and
> New American Library bring new hope to young
> writers: Publishers will publish *anything*, every-
> thing, everyone, anybody, *tout le monde*, ragtag and
> bobtail. What's more, you can depend on critics,
> who can always be counted on to behave like ladies
> and gentlemen, to stand reverently, hands clasped
> upon their bosoms, around any old literary Pamper
> you poop in, and exclaim, "Gloria in excelsis Deo!"
> Let me state at the outset that I am neither a lady
> nor a—praise the lord!—gentleman. Wiping my
> butt with these two books is a fate far more majes-
> tic than they deserve.
>
> But wipe I did and—a true son of his mother—
> flushed, only to discover that—behold!—my pot
> runneth over!

It seems almost impossible that this ferocious gangster of a critic could have emerged, like a phoenix, from the wan, exquisite poet who used to describe such things as "the Sunday bells ringing again, slowly ringing, in such a sad, knowing voice that tells of great depth and of my life that rings as sadly and as deeply." The brutality of this complex scatological image represents the mirror opposite of the excesses of the diaries, whose rhetoric I now repudiated in a classic instance of self-disavowal. Whereas I once used metaphors for purposes of beautification, I now use them for purposes of "uglification," to degrade and deflate my subject as I plunge my scalpel into novels I vivisect without anesthesia, delighting in the screams of my innocent, if entirely deserving, victims. Interestingly enough, I am still writing in the elocutionary mode, addressing unseen participants with such asides as "behold!," "praise the lord!," and "a true son of his mother." But unlike the diaries, in which my poetic recitations took place under the illusion of solitude, as if I were talking to myself in an empty room and the reader listening with his ear cupped against the door, I am now once again, as in my early letters, speaking to a real audience, which I hammer with punch lines like a stand-up comic on a smoke-filled stage. Declamation has given way to talking, gabbing, bitching, as in the following characteristically ruthless summary of Arnold Peyser's novel, *The Squirrelcage*:

> The whole awful world of barbarous adults, evil stepfathers, sadistic doctors, perverted orderlies, and sundry other meanies would like to prove that poor little barmy Paul Martin in Arnold Peyser's *The Squirrelcage* is mad as a March Hare—and just because he put glass in the cupcakes, slashed his father's tires, beat the shit out of his mother, and swallowed a bottle of Bayer. But Paul's not really such a bad person underneath it all, even if he did set the house on fire and constantly imperiled the physical well-being of those around him. He just needed Someone to Love. And that's where Ruth

> comes in — a crusading social worker at the local
> booby hatch who believes in Paul and who mumbles,
> with the transfixed gaze of the brain-dead, eerie
> incantations like "You're afraid to deal with *now*," or,
> even more cryptically, "Did you ever think that *you*
> are your own place?" Thrice around she weaves her
> spell, whereupon after weeks of "group" and months
> of getting in touch with anger, Paul's eyes glaze over,
> his feet shuffle, and he, too, begins to sputter the
> same sort of cabalistic nonsense. Soon, feeling much
> better about himself, he returns home (best of luck
> to you, Mrs. Martin!), a brand-new person.

As part of this project of self-demolition, my new style actively incorporates aspects of my former personae, which it mercilessly parodies, turning what was once a series of childish mannerisms into a shtick, a hilarious gag that I now use like a practical joke, a surefire method for getting a laugh. Although cracking with age, the solemn voice of Jeeves has emerged again, still demeaning his sister after all this time with such portentous phrases as "to your satisfaction" and "inspire a convivial mood," language that once elevated me over my family but that now has become an essential feature of my ironic mask, of the deadpan formality with which I discuss, for comic purposes, matters of utter triviality. Take the opening paragraph of a review of *Facts and Phalluses*, a collection of lore about penises:

> Alexandra Parsons's entertaining gallop through
> the facts and fictions surrounding a subject of such

gravity and import as men's dirty little pee things
contains information that Mother never told you,
not only about the birds and the bees, but about the
beavers and the armadillos, the four-eyed anableps
and the Abyssinian bats. Seasoned veterans
amongst us have always known, from hearsay if not
hands-on experience, that the "inexpressibles" (to
use Edward Gibbon's polite euphemism) are hard
and long and, to the faint of heart, unutterably terrifying. But bony, barbed, bristled, webbed, forked,
hooked, and hacksaw-edged?! One can only imagine that, in the course of what has almost certainly
been a long and unhappy career, Parsons has had
some *very* unfortunate experiences.

Once again, I resort to preposterous circumlocutions:
"gravity and import," "seasoned veterans amongst us,"
and "unutterably terrifying," poetic phraseology culled
from the fiction of Charlotte Brontë or the essays of
Samuel Johnson, the most inappropriate literary models
possible for a discussion of the "inexpressibles." The
grandiloquence that was once involuntary, the reflexive
tic of an insecure kid who used language to define himself
against his homophobic environment, has become a cunning and deliberate form of theater in which I resurrect
Jeeves from the dead. My old linguistic habits reappear in
quotation marks, as the basic components of a new style
created out of calculated self-satire.

This largely unconscious process of revisiting my former
mannerisms constitutes a new method of self-construction,

one based, not on the appropriation of the writings of others, but on the appropriation and perversion of my own writings. Turning away from the sacred texts of the gurus for whom I once operated as a higher sort of belletristic channeler, I continued the task of building my distinctive voice by engaging in an elaborate self-excavation in which I doubled back on myself and retraced my literary history. Much as I once projected my pretentiousness onto the rest of the Oberlin student body, so I projected my disgust with the unhinged figure of the diaries onto the dreck I reviewed. In my early reviews, I killed two birds with one stone: on the surface, I appear to be dissecting the authors of bad gay novels, which entirely deserved the treatment I gave them, but, unconsciously, I am actually dissecting myself, reexamining aspects of my style that I found so disgraceful that I was incapable of facing them directly. In this complicated method of self-correction, the book under review functioned as a psychological buffer that protected me from feeling the full heat of an act in which I burned my former style like a heretic at the stake, using another writer as an unfortunate surrogate, who was made to pay, not only for his own sins, but for mine as well.

Two aspects of the style of the diaries in particular were subjected to this circuitous route of self-criticism: my philosophizing and my priggishness about sex. Compare the following two passages, the first from the diaries and the second from a review of Andrew Harvey's *The Web*, a novel full of the kind of mysticism found in the notebooks:

What have I seen in these past two days? I have
seen the sublime power of my soul. I have watched
myself move through time like a gust of wind. I am
part of a whole which pulses to such beautiful
music. I feel as if I had taken the sky for a brother
and I was as large and distant as the stars at night.
The people around me are a part of this whole, too;
I wish that I could make them see what large and
mysterious lives they lead. My life is immense and
mysterious. I am as noble as the sky. I've felt a certain grace in each one of my movements that speaks
to me of some higher union of body and soul. If we
could all feel that we danced and, when we spoke,
that we sang and, when we thought, that we
weaved, our lives would be immeasurably deeper
than they are now.

Andrew Harvey's *The Web* belongs to that genre
of crap in which wicked lounge lizards, reclining on
Louis Quinze sofas, nibble *oeufs au jambon*, toss
stoles over kimonos, "refresh" themselves with
Maria Callas recordings, and, when hysterical,
screech "How do you know my mother had fits of
madness?" Adolphe, a famous (why not?)
transvestite film director, is dying, Egypt, dying. In
the middle of his elaborate last rites, just before
he — and the reader — are about to be anointed with
extreme unctuousness, Charles, his minion, [and]
their mutual friend Anna, an artiste of the same
stripe, [seek out] the company of Tibetan monks
and Indian messiahs and travel abroad in search of

themselves and the Meaning of Life and the
Meaning of Death and the meaning of this and the
meaning of that and the meaning of boop-boop-pee-
do and blah, blah, blah—only to discover that all
the world is just a *Web* of many-colored threads
which knit and weave a holistic unity of organic
beauty and oneness. . . . As part of his preparation
for death, Adolphe meets up with a Tibetan monk
who, in addition to chaperoning the other characters' out-of-body experiences, tells about one occasion in which he had a mystic revelation while sitting on—I kid you not—the toilet: "My body
spread over the whole world. It had ceased to be
solid. It had become a series of pulsing waves."
Now some would call this a mystical experience,
but I call it . . . diarrhea.

The second passage could almost stand as a close reading of the first. I used the improbable medium of the book
review as a covert form of therapy in which all of my negative reviews merged into one immense pan of the single
execrable book that hovers behind all of my pieces, constituting their real target, the archetypal bad novel, the
touchstone of atrociousness: my journals.

The same sort of dialogue occurs between the cynical
things I said about sex in sappy gay novels, in which every
private, physical act inevitably becomes a public, propa-
gandistic one, and the childish things I said about sex in
the diaries (as when I apologized in all earnestness to a
reproduction I kept over my bed of Leonardo da Vinci's

Ginevra for performing the unspeakably degenerate act of masturbating in her presence). Compare the following quotations, the first from an entry in the diaries, which recounts my feelings of guilt after having slept with a man I picked up at a gay dance, and the second from the reviews:

> I feel stained—I am soiled—I have brought myself down once again. I feel as if I had lost my soul. I have gone astray . . . and placed myself up for men's appraisal. . . . I sorrow for this night and deep is my regret. . . . Someday it may be my fortune to know a man as self-contained and enchanted as myself, and we will have simple and eternal love.

> As with most "think" books, the sex scenes [in Tom Wakefield's *Mates*] are handled with maidenly reserve, the author's sermonizing reaching hilarious extremes when "special moments," as he calls them, are being relished. Rarely involving any form of penetration (the butt, let alone the cock, being entirely off limits in this kind of true-love ballet), "think" sex is usually presented through the rose-colored glasses of Feelings, Very Special Feelings. Beds seldom shake or bodies thrash in this genre, the bed being the marital bower and the body the anointed temple through which lifetime commitments are consecrated. On the very few occasions in the book when casual sex actually occurs, Wakefield tsks, tsks, tsks and cluck, cluck, clucks with Schlaflyite fervor.

In the passage from the diaries, I describe myself as a defenseless waif, a beseeching innocent with wide-open eyes standing forlorn and abandoned in a big bad world of rapacious brutes whose unseemly advances I unsuccessfully fend off by brandishing, like Little Bo Peep, my shepherdess's crook. In my literary criticism, however, this virginal maiden, whose implausibility is almost grotesque, is trotted out like a broken marionette in book review after book review, where her sniveling puritanism is repeatedly unmasked as the cant of a hypocritical prude.

In my first experiences as a commercial writer, my confrontation with a live audience that needed to be constantly entertained enabled me to extricate myself from the unreadably self-involved style of the solipsist. But the intoxicating discovery of a genuine readership jeopardized my identity as a writer in a new and dangerous way, posing a completely different threat to my style than that presented by the diaries' ghost readership. From the introverted extremes of my early years, I was led to the extroverted extremes of the blustering monologuist, the court jester, an unlikely role for a cloistered poet. The result was a maniacal tendency to overwrite. Attempting to make every inch of syntax count, I composed in units no larger than the individual clause. When clustered together, these bright, glittering images undermined the structure of my essays until each piece disintegrated into a series of discrete verbal events, none of which bore the slightest relation to any other. In an analysis of a reissue of the nineteenth-century melodrama *East Lynne*, for instance, I indulged in the jewel-encrusted style into which I still frequently lapse, stating that "while half a million Victorians gnashed their teeth and pulled their pigtails with every yank of its soap-operatics, now in the 1980s the book makes only the feeblest tug of a tear-jerk on the *Dallas*-sodden noodles of our heartstrings."

But just when it looked as if I would never disentangle myself from my mixed metaphors, displacement once again came to my rescue. Even as my prose congealed into epic similes that grew more and more outlandish, I displayed absolute intolerance for the overwriting of others whose prose allowed me to study my own shortcomings at several removes, from a vantage point far above the vendetta I was waging as the self-appointed hatchet man of minority fiction. Often I was so blind to my tendency to write purple prose that I overwrote in the very act of criticizing overwriting, as in a review of a re-release of the Nobel Laureate Patrick White's novel *The Aunt's Story*, in which I complained that such " 'creative' writers [as White] tack up their prose before us like —en garde! —a frilly valance or a swatch of gaudy brocade"; or when I praised Patricia Highsmith, who, unlike other American writers, was so committed to telling her story that she never had "any time to single out something for its own sake, to pluck it up from its context, and pet it from head to toe with long, voluptuous strokes of adjectives and metaphors." Far from being smug about my skills as a writer, I was bitterly frustrated, divided between my need

– 41 –

to entertain my audience and my abhorrence of the prose that resulted from my acrobatic efforts to maintain my readers' interest. The development of my writing up until the present has been a matter of walking this fine line, reining in my desire to overwrite without at the same time sacrificing the liveliness and animation that originated in my liberating awareness of a physical audience in every way harder to please and less trustworthy than the imaginary audience of posterity. Throughout my history as a writer, from Jeeves to the anchoress to the gangster, the major changes in my prose have occurred as the result of a strong undercurrent of self-disgust, which still courses beneath the surface of my style and which has always exerted a positive influence on my development, on the one hand freeing me from the claustrophobia of the diaries and, on the other, preventing me from becoming subservient to a commercial audience that would deprive me of my autonomy.

When I look back at the self-mutilation that I have performed in the course of a chapter in which I have dragged all of my skeletons out of my closet and stood eyeball to eyeball with the entire crew of my past selves, a comment comes to mind that Arthur Koestler made in his memoir, *The Invisible Writing*. Here, he warned the autobiographer that the impulse towards sincerity easily degenerates into exhibitionism, so that all of the "episodes that should be embarrassing and painful to tell are told with wallowing gusto." It is true, of course, that I have failed to check the impulse towards sincerity and have been guilty of "wallowing," but when I think of the reluctance with which most writers look back at their early work, only to slam the book shut as soon as their eyes alight on the incriminating passages they unfailingly find, I feel that there is something valuable about serving myself up like a specimen on a platter, skewered and sutured and stuffed, an anatomical display that I offer as a kind of corrective to the habitual reticence with which people discuss their literary development. Writers as a tribe loathe the paper trail that has led them to their present position and cannot bear to examine the cast-off identities they leave strewn in their wakes as they try on one ill-fitting costume after another. In fact, this horror of looking back at the work that paved the way to the present is so instinctive that writers are, ironically, the worst book burners around, systematically effacing their traces, altering the record, destroying the diaries, hiding the evidence, all in an effort to pretend that they have not changed, have not developed, were always exactly as you find them now, having sprung like Athena from Zeus's head, fully formed and armed to the teeth. We attempt to deceive others into believing that we have remained static as writers from the beginning, that there was no self-experimentation, no posing, no lying, no insincerity, that we were born with a fully evolved style—an illusion we cling to, presiding over our reputations as if we were our own bodyguards, our own curators, the executors of our own carefully bowdlerized estates.

Some of this shame stems no doubt from a belief central to the Judeo-Christian tradition that we are born with a clearly defined character and that any attempt to become someone else, to imitate Thoreau or Lao-tse or Kierke-gaard or even poor Jeeves, represents an unpardonable act of self-betrayal, of disloyalty to some kind of God-given soul or temperament. But because neither our per-sonalities nor our prose styles are emanations of an intrin-sic sensibility, such a view seriously misrepresents the task of self-construction, which invariably involves insincerity and impersonation, the petty thefts we make when we mimic those who have a stronger sense of selfhood than we do. To believe otherwise, to burn our diaries, to turn our backs on the selves that we have been and pretend that we have always had the same monolithic, unchanging style, is the ultimate act of self-betrayal, the ultimate imposture, one far more ludicrous and insincere than the poses I struck in my diaries.

It is difficult to have compassion for oneself, to make peace with the voices that are still speaking in one's style. In a moment of unusual foresight when I was eighteen, I once imagined what it would be like to read my diaries when I was older:

> I wonder if I shall ever reread these words again,
> and if so what I shall think of them when I am old
> and wise. What shall I see in my foolishness? I will
> surely be kind to my youth, for you see I am so
> afraid I will be unkind to myself when I am old and

wise, and that I shall disown what is rightfully
mine—this foolish blind youth, this inarticulate
clumsy youth of mine.

I was always writing for posterity, and now at last,
some twenty-five years later, I have become posterity.
Although it would be asking too much for me to forgive
my former excesses, I find that my heart goes out to this
strange creature from the past and I find myself replying
that, while I cannot be kind, I will not disown what is
rightfully mine, this foolish blind youth, this inarticulate
clumsy youth of mine.

3

Dressing

Closets for me are not for clothes. They are for papers, old phone books, mops, stationery supplies, winter blankets, receipts for taxes, and broken umbrellas. Like a traveler who lives out of his suitcase, cramming everything from his passport to his toothbrush into a light-weight tote bag and then dashing for the next plane, I live almost entirely out of my bureau, which contains hundreds of T-shirts, briefs, and pairs of socks, none of which I ever fold but instead wad up like rags and pack into drawers so crowded that I can close them only by means of a swift bump with my hip. Nothing I own needs to be hung on hangers, let alone ironed, dry-cleaned, tailored, or even washed on the "gentle" cycle — no expensive Italian suits, no neatly creased dress pants, no dapper blue blazers, but only mountains of graying undershirts and several months' worth of holey white socks.

Since I spend almost the entire day alone, I am by nature a nudist, a slatternly idler who lounges about in little more than a nightshirt spattered with coffee stains and an effeminate pair of satin slippers which, along with a full-length crimson robe made of sumptuous velour, add an incongruous touch of decadent aesthete to my appearance. I seldom dress before noon and, because my clothes are so tight, undress as early in the day as my conscience allows, guiltily slipping into my evening attire at the unseemly hour of 5 or 6 P.M., already settling in with a novel for a night of solitude sitting in my recliner. Whenever I return from the gym or the grocery store, I immediately remove my pants and shirt so that I am constantly dressing and undressing, trying on this T-shirt, squeezing into those cut-off shorts, putting on that pair of blue Pro-Keds, like an actor forced to play several parts, no sooner donning one disguise than rushing backstage to put on another—although in my case each costume is identical, each character the same character, that of a laid-back gay baby boomer who, when he bothers to dress at all, wears nothing more stylish than Levis and Reeboks.

As a victim of a fierce Protestant Clothing Ethic (my distrust of frivolous ornaments is so intense that I have thoroughly de-accessorized myself, refusing to wear watches, rings, belts, baseball caps, or even sunglasses), I am plagued by inflexible notions of authenticity, by the uncompromising belief that I must be the same person at all times, regardless of the occasion. Despite what I professed in "Writing," I return to a static conception of the self incompatible with the whole sport of dressing up in masquerade and taking on alternative identities, flitting from the tramp to the bohemian intellectual to the modish man-about-town. And yet while I reject on both political and moral grounds the consumeristic myth that fashion enables us to explore multiple personalities through subtle alterations in our appearance, my righteous pretense of authenticity is in fact a lie in that everything about my clothing is inauthentic. I am a crafty plagiarist who, like a scavenger on a battlefield, cobbles together his wardrobe from other people's clothing: from the outfits of the athlete, whose jerseys and tennis shoes I buy; from the footwear of the construction worker, whose boots I put on when I cruise; from the uniforms of the soldier, whose camouflage fatigues I acquire at army and navy stores; and even from the lingerie of the businessman, whose pristine white Jockey shorts suggest to me the unstudied masculinity of someone well above the fray of gay underwear fetishism (what's more, this icon of virility possesses an incontrovertible badge of maleness, a live-in laundress, his wife, who lovingly maintains—and even purchases— the most intimate articles of his impeccably clean wardrobe). Although my entire life occurs indoors sitting at my desk or in my recliner, I wear the clothing of a rugged, outdoorsy type of guy who spends his time digging the foundations of skyscrapers in the hot sun or operating ten-story cranes and hydraulic forklifts, not the preciously aesthetic garb of an intellectual who lives alone in a quiet room, reading, taking notes, and sipping coffee.

Nowhere is the inauthenticity of my wardrobe seen more clearly than in the contrast between my work shoes and the construction boots I wear for cruising. When I am typing at the law firm on a weekday, I make only perfunctory attempts to keep within the boundaries of the office dress code, wearing a battered pair of leather Rockports, which are in fact little more than glorified tennis shoes. I never untie them but use them like slippers. I even exercise in them when I am at the gym, abusing them during such strenuous workouts on the StairMaster that their backs have collapsed, their sides have cracked and split, their treads have disappeared, and their soles are so abraded that they slope sharply to the right. My shoes are not well-polished Oxfords that I squeeze into with a shoe horn and tie in a neat bow, but ripped, discolored sneakers that are trying unsuccessfully to "pass" as business shoes, much as I myself am trying unsuccessfully to "pass" as a secretary, all the while fully aware that I am an interloper here, that I am in disguise, and not a very effective disguise at that. Since my everyday wardrobe is intimately linked to my homosexuality, wearing the faded Permapress shirts and unflattering polyester pants that I purchase at bargain-basement prices attacks the very core of my identity and emasculates me entirely, especially when I am throttled by a tie, the only form of tight clothing I am unable to tolerate.

My sex shoes involve another act of self-betrayal, although a far more exhilarating one. While exuding an air of sturdy preparedness for back-breaking manual labor, these indestructible boots are in almost perfect condition, having never been used as they were intended but only for such safe and untaxing recreational activities as stomping through the underbrush of cruise parks or slinking through the orgy rooms of sex clubs. Because we often hate our own work and feel degraded by it, it is always someone else's work clothes that are sexy, someone else's uniform, never our own, and the construction worker would be as likely to wear *my* shoes on a date as I am to wear *his* when I dress up in the drag of the lumpen proletariat and rampage through the bushes. My democratic sensitivity to the distastefulness of pulling rank with my clothing dovetails perfectly with my need to acquire the sexual charisma of the blue-collar worker, who has become a font of male iconography for effeminate homosexuals, an unwitting trendsetter for those who worship such symbols of virility as the tool belts of carpenters, the flannel shirts of lumberjacks, and the leather chaps of ranch hands. My need to establish visual allegiance to the unwashed peasant may stem from my liberal upbringing, but it is not as disinterestedly political as it might at first appear, since donning their clothing also endows me with their machismo, which I use for my own parasitic purposes at the same time that I inevitably patronize them as brutish simpletons.

– 51 –

There are, however, strict limits to my playful allusions to blue-collar dress. My body is divided into a map of irreconcilably contentious regions, each of which has its own aesthetic, one pertaining to what I wear below my neck and one to what I wear above: namely, my glasses, which I have chosen intentionally to give me a look of professorial studiousness, the owlish intensity of a near-sighted don blinded by a lifetime of reading. Because I view my face as the very center of my individuality and even the outward manifestation of my subjective life, it is one of the only places on my body where I refuse to dress in masquerade, where I insist on maintaining complete authenticity and projecting a look more suited to my actual interests and profession. Given that I have attempted to eliminate the look of the intellectual in every other aspect of my wardrobe, it is odd that I cultivate it so vigorously above the neck, even refusing to wear contact lenses. Since my face is too close to my real sense of identity to carry on the game I play elsewhere, I have turned myself into a kind of biological collage, a Frankenstein of mismatched parts, with a sensitive, "poetic" head grafted on to a bloated, muscular body.

The aesthetic that governs my glasses also governs the left side of this collage, the shoulder on which I carry my book bag, a cumbersome leather satchel that hangs around my neck like a millstone and bulges with volumes of philosophy and art history so heavy that their weight often chafes my skin. I would never consider harnessing myself into a vinyl backpack, a hideous accessory that suggests to me bright-eyed-and-bushy-tailed undergraduates hiking over mountain trails, the very picture of rugged heterosexual wholesomeness. Instead, because my bag contains the tools of my trade, much as my eyes are essential to my literary pursuits, I have chosen a strappy, over-the-shoulder pocketbook that suggests the opposite of the manly persona I create with my tight jeans and T-shirts: European sophistication, a quality with which these bags are historically linked, given that "male purses," as they were once known, first became fashionable in Europe in the late 1960s and were only begrudgingly accepted by American men, who were at first flabbergasted by the sight of otherwise "normal" males sashaying down the streets swinging expensive designer creations by Gucci and Louis Vuitton.

Having reached the ripe old age of forty-three, I find myself on the very threshold of that awkward period in which one begins to dress far too young for one's years and passersby stare rudely at one's scantily clad body, which offers such a vivid contrast to one's haggard face and receding hairline. My boyfriends have been unsparingly candid in their judgment of my shorty-shorts, A-shirts, and high-top sneakers, which embarrass them as much as husbands are ashamed of wives well past their prime who wear hot pants and miniskirts. It is not, however, as if I am actively imitating the styles of young people whose fads in clothing have no appeal to me, relishing as I do the psychic advantages of maturity and disliking the way in which teenagers conform to the pack, defining themselves as a tribe by means of their Adidas sweatpants and Abercrombie and Fitch gym shorts. My own outfits are not devolving, regressing, returning to childhood; they have simply refused to change for over twenty years. Though my body has aged, my hair has fallen out in clumps, and my stomach muscles have slackened, my clothing came to a complete standstill sometime during my college years, the tail end of the disco era where, an ageless and immutable atavism, I still reside.

This extraordinary inertia is the result not only of the anxiety of a dowdy, premenopausal homosexual trying desperately to lop decades off his actual physical age but also of the fact that, unlike most educated people who have pursued respectable careers in the business world, I have chosen a vocation whose privacy has enabled me to look exactly as I did when I was a student. Having no pressing reason to change my wardrobe, no need to dress up for the client luncheon or the urgent meeting in the boardroom, I am imprisoned like Endymion in a type of eternal youth, which has turned me into an unsightly anachronism strangely immune to the continual series of fashion updates that people make as they move from one high-paying job to the next. Far from attempting to reju- venate myself with my clothing by modeling myself on the gangly adolescent tormented by his squeaky voice, grow- ing pains, and pimples, I am the ultimate stick-in-the- mud, a taxidermic specimen, an old fogey whose life is so unvarying that he has never bothered to modernize his fashions.

The stagnant nature of my dress is also related to the AIDS epidemic, which has robbed gay fashion of its whole raison d'être as a uniform expressly designed for cruising the meat rack. Deprived of one of my major pastimes, I have fallen prey to the Miss Havisham syndrome, still wearing my bridal gown for a ceremony that never occurred, my clock stopped at the very moment the Centers for Disease Control issued their first chilling advisory. Rather than putting our cowboy boots, rawhide vests, and skintight chaps out to pasture, gay men now wear them to remind themselves that they are still sexual beings, however dangerous it is to act on our impulses. Dressing provocatively has become a substitute for sex and buoys up my despondent libido, which, clinging nostalgically to the old costumes, is always in a high state of military preparedness, ready to return to the front lines at a moment's notice. My outfits did not change to meet the new challenges I faced but slipped into a time warp where I still remain expectantly, waiting for the cure, fully intending to hurl my naked body back into an orgy after a twenty-year intermission.

AIDS has also increased the importance of the health club in my life. Although I am annoyingly self-righteous about refusing to dress up for formal occasions, I am quite willing to dress up for *in*formal ones, specifically, an activity that few people besides homosexuals would ever consider dressing up for, namely, exercising at the gym, a routine that brings out in most heterosexuals the negligent slob who mopes around unhappily in sweatshirts and gym trunks that balloon around his knees. Unlike my fellow "physical culturists" who view the gym as a necessary evil, I view it as a stage, a catwalk on which to parade in sexy outfits, striking poses in body-hugging Lycra suits that dismay sweating heterosexuals hyperventilating on the treadmill and slogging through their butt-buster classes in clammy leotards. During the 1980s and 1990s, Lycra became for me a real live body condom, a miraculous textile onto which I displaced my libido, which found some relief from the torments of celibacy in the sheer act of exhibitionism, in strutting my stuff at the lat-pull machine or the squat rack. In the only conscious act of transvestism I have engaged in in my life, I now routinely buy my gym outfits from the women's department of sporting goods stores, not because I want to look girlish, but because women's trunks are much shorter than men's and thus allow me to expose a few more centimeters of the muscular hams I have suffered so keenly to develop. Near-desperate store clerks do everything in their power to steer me out of the "ladies'" section, as if I were an obscene panty sniffer who delighted in fondling sports bras and tennis skirts.

The gym is one of the only places where I actually wear clothing out-of-doors, since, as a writer, I spend most of my time alone, protected by a solitude that has made me so shameless that I gallivant about naked in front of windows that open directly onto a busy street where mothers stroll past pushing perambulators and children make their maiden voyages on bikes with training wheels. Amidst my quiet library and modern conveniences, I am reverting to the edenic immodesty of the naked savage who performs his most vital functions in full view of the tribe, decked out in little more than a leopard-skin *cache-sexe*. The desocializing reclusiveness of the writer is just as conducive to nakedness as the public life of the hunter-gatherer scrabbling for roots in his birthday suit. In nakedness, the savage and the intellectual meet on common ground, sharing the same fig leaf, joining hands in the altogether, a state that is at once the most primitive and the most civilized, the most wild-and-woolly and the most finically cosmopolitan.

For a would-be naked savage, however, I have the largest collection of loincloths in the Western Hemisphere. One of the strange pathologies of my wardrobe is that I am unable to throw anything out and am therefore saddled with a huge vault of moldering rags that I have owned, if not worn, for decades. I labor under the misconception that I must maintain a huge stockpile of white T-shirts because one day I may want to wear exactly *that* white T-shirt, which is virtually identical to every other white T-shirt I own, give or take a few coffee stains and yellowing perspiration marks. The need for variety as an excuse for hoarding clothing is another of the great lies of my wardrobe, since everything I own is a carbon copy of every other garment and could be replaced for pennies, even though I persist in seeing the most prosaic brand names as unique and somehow expressive of my personality, despite the fact that every man in America is wearing the same Hanes V-necks and combed-cotton BVDs.

There are two explanations for my irrational tendency to hoard superannuated undergarments. In a consumerist society characterized by instantaneous obsolescence, I have never developed sufficiently strong instincts for discarding things and treat my acquisitions exactly as I would sturdier items from another era, which were designed to last for longer periods of time, promoting habits of possessiveness that have placed an enormous strain on the limited closet space of the modern house and apartment.

What's more, as a man of slender means, I enjoy the act of shopping as wholeheartedly as any Park Avenue millionaire, but, rather than rolling my cart up and down the aisles of Barneys and Bergdorf Goodman, I must make do with the dusty merchandise of close-out stores, buying the same generic white T-shirt over and over again, no sooner tearing off the plastic from a package of Fruit of the Looms than I feel an overwhelming compulsion to squander my weekly allowance on an even costlier set of Calvin Kleins. The fact that these insignificant impulse purchases have so little variety shows how symbolic consumption is for me, since the commodity itself is irrelevant, the real source of enjoyment being my low-budget crawl through bargain basements, where I rummage through bins of "imperfect" shopworn goods, their prices slashed for inventory clearance. Consumption attains in me a higher level of abstraction than it does in most people. And yet the petty purchases I make on these economical larks are motivated by the same consumer psychology that leads a du Pont or a Rothschild to buy his own version of the white T-shirt, sinking fortunes into Ferraris and Rembrandts, engaging in the sport of splurging as an avocation in itself, a game in which the closet is simply a depository of the useless spoils of obsessive spending sprees.

Like so many self-involved adolescents, I once vainly (and, it goes without saying, quite erroneously) believed that I was a knockout and dressed accordingly to set off my smashing good looks, which I felt deserved lovely clothing to exhibit my radiance to its fullest advantage. In my early twenties, pride took a great spill, my cheeks (all four of them) lost their youthful bloom, and my hair fell out, first slowly, then with the inexorability of a tide ebbing away from my temples and soon receding from my entire forehead. A shadow of the Adonis I once was, I felt the source of my power gradually shift downwards from my features to my physique, which I recreated through weight lifting in the image of a generic male archetype, gaining fifty pounds on high-caloric cafeteria food and undertaking a grueling new aerobics regimen. I began to realize that being sexy is not about attracting attention, not about *expressing* myself, but about *suppressing* myself, eliminating idiosyncrasies, reducing myself to the featureless male, a barrel-chested Everyman whose appeal lies in his ability to embody that most commonplace and stereotyped of qualities, masculinity. As I lost my facial vanity and acquired my muscles, my clothes were the first casualty of my disillusionment with the whole concept of individuality, for who would want to hide in billowing shirts and loose-fitting trousers the iconic male form that I had struggled so hard to achieve? Having worked out for over twenty years, I now realize that my real wardrobe is not my T-shirt collection but my body itself, which is a type of prosthetic suit that shields the effeminate gay man from sexual ostracism and enables me to be as promiscuous as I want to be without significantly altering my attitudes or behavior. Looking masculine saves me from a far worse fate, a far worse concession to society: *being* masculine. While some would say that I treat my body in an alienated way, jerking it about like a marionette on a stick, this piece of bionic camouflage has actually liberated me, conserved my mental energies, and isolated the damaging effects of conformity by confining it to my body, which I have sacrificed with no compunction whatsoever to the gods of social expectations in order to protect the freedom of my internal life.

Now in my forties, rents have developed in my prosthetic suit, its elbows have worn thin; my complexion is no longer smooth and unblemished, my ass is collapsing, there are dimples on my thighs, hair is sprouting from my ears and nostrils, my eyes and mouth are surrounded by the deep crevices of laugh lines, and a small beer gut has long outworn its welcome, no matter how conscientiously I diet. As my body becomes harder to maintain, I find myself entering what may be the final stage in the evolution of my wardrobe: the burial of the bionic body and the triumphant return of textiles. I have begun to buy clothing specifically for comfort and actually to conceal what remains of my physique: baggy pullovers in bright colors, deliciously soft terry cloth house robes, flannel pajamas, cozy slippers, and pants several inches wider than my actual waist size. My involvement with my clothing is becoming increasingly antisocial, based on a selfish new interest in the pure sensuality of fabrics, colors, and patterns, which I have begun to enjoy—not out of vanity, as a way of setting off the good looks I am perfectly aware I have lost, but as ends in themselves, as sources of pleasure that I enjoy in an exclusively aesthetic way. For my entire life, clothing has served a communicative function and dressing has involved a shouting match with an imaginary audience, a dialogue in which I am still embroiled, still outing myself to heterosexuals, still showing my disdain for formal wear, still expressing my sympathies for the prole, and, most important, still vamping for the galleries, batting my eyes and moueing at men like an aging prostitute. And yet there are unmistakable signs that the whole nature of the dialogue is changing and that my interlocutor has left the room forever, abandoning me to a state of splendid isolation in which I fully intend to sit myself down for a nice long heart-to-heart, not with potential suitors, but—at last—with myself.

4

Laughing

A formative experience in the development of my sense of humor occurred in the third or fourth grade when my mother recorded a tape in which she described in colorful detail how, exasperated with the irritations of raising a family and anxious to do her part in curbing the population explosion, she tried to murder her three children. She struck my sister Lynn on the head with an ax, but Lynn's skull blunted the blade, and the bullet ricocheted off my spine when she shot me point-blank in the back with a pistol, a blow I received with frightening imperturbability, mentioning only in passing, "Mama, I have a little pain in my back." Disappointed by these bungled attempts, she arranged for Lee to be bumped off by a gang of hired thugs; but they proved no match for my hyperactive sister, already a brown belt at the age of thirteen, who kicked her assailants unconscious and returned home in high dudgeon to complain (in the characteristically homophobic manner of her tomboy adolescence), "Mama, three sissy-fems set upon me in the woods."

Years later, while working in the day care center my mother ran, I amused my coworkers by narrating the tragic deaths of the children milling around us on the playground — Stephen, who would accidentally hang himself with his jump rope while swinging from the monkey bars; Mary, who would dive to the bottom of the wading pool in search of her cat's-eye marble, never to resurface from its unhygienic depths; Bob, who would break his neck on the teeter-totter after being lobbed over the jungle gym like a stone from a catapult; and Cindy, who would be dragged to her death in the gravel, the strap of her pinafore entangled in the merry-go-round. Virtually from infancy, I was nursed on the toxic milk of my mother's gallows humor, a Morticia Adams's morbidity that shattered taboos and scoffed at the innocence of children, the benevolence of God, the greatness of America, and even the sanctity of motherhood itself. Once, she greeted me after school wearing a long blond wig, her face made up like a whore's, blowing smoke rings while leaning suggestively against her bedroom door, waggling her finger invitingly in my direction and saying, "Come here, come over here, big boy."

Her perverse gaiety has, since childhood, led me to blur — indeed, erase altogether — the line between the joke and the insult. I compulsively taunt the people around me, whether by jeering at the ostensible insignificance of my friend Joaquin's two scholarly works, which I claim will be used not to further the research of other medievalists but to help out housewives, who will put the volumes to work as doorstops and props to keep windows open (hence the titles I have given them, *Window Prop Number 1* and *Window Prop Number 2*); or by grabbing the phone whenever a coworker walks into the room and pretending to be talking with her husband, with whom I claim to be carrying on a torrid affair, laughing about her dreadful cooking, dowdiness, and vulgar tastes, and cackling like a hyena as I plead, "But no, no, no, José, you mustn't, it isn't right, it isn't fair, we shouldn't make fun of the poor thing like this, she can't help it."

Humor for me almost invariably involves a mock attack in which I impersonate a nasty bitch, a frequently irksome ritual that is the exact linguistic equivalent of tickling, of parents who dig their fingers into their children's ribs while snapping their teeth like cannibals and roaring, "I am going to eat you up." Arrested at this distressingly infantile stage of development, my sense of humor has never evolved much further beyond the game of chase or peek-a-boo, of putting on what one acquaintance has called my "wicked-stepmother expression" and laughing about Joaquin's tribal artifacts collection, which I dismiss as a set of amateurish forgeries made by unscrupulous black women on the other side of Flatbush Avenue from trees they chop down in Prospect Park ("I hear that old queen on President Street needs another Yoruba divination bowl!"). Tickling appeals to me, not only because it brings to mind the gentle mauling I received from my mother but also because it is a form of humor that requires familiarity and trust (to say nothing of a great deal of patience), a mutual understanding so complete that friends can instantaneously decipher deliberately misleading statements and interpret my aggression and hostility as their exact opposite, as affection, as kisses in the disguise of slaps, caresses that resemble pinches. Children often cry when they are tickled by strangers, unable to perceive the difference between aggression and playfulness, a distinction that becomes clear to them only when they realize that that savage gnashing his teeth and lunging for their ribs has no intention of really pulling off their noses or gnawing on their toes. Even as adults, we are frightened by strangers. I incorporate this deep-seated distrust of other people into my daily behavior, evoking the threat of attack and then immediately withdrawing it, inspiring both relief at a false alarm and intimacy as one learns the rules of the game and overcomes the reflex to flinch from oncoming blows. Every joke I make is an epistemological experiment in which I gauge my forbearing audience's I.Q. in irony, its ability to discern the difference between corny gibes that become ever more vicious as my targets build up tolerance to my perpetual needling, and angry affronts that, on very infrequent occasions, are really intended to insult and humiliate.

Amassing a body of private jokes is another way of intensifying intimacy, the development of what Natalia

Ginzburg has called "the family lexicon." Old friends almost always build up over time an arcane language of untranslatable references, code words and secret handshakes that, because they depend on shared experiences, are seldom funny to outsiders, as in the case of one of Joaquin's favorite expressions, "bojangles," meaning "superb," as in "That book was really bojangles" and "Didn't you think the Chardin show was utterly bojangles?" The word entered our private vocabulary by way of my mother, who during a telephone conversation mentioned in passing a typically Southern restaurant named Bojangles, a greasy spoon whose barbecued chicken she ate every week, virtually slobbering into the receiver as she explained that "it's real, real spicy; we *LIKE* it down here." I described to Joaquin how she had smacked her lips with obscene gusto as she recalled the taste of her favorite treat, whereupon he adopted the word as an inappropriate expression for any number of highbrow hankerings, from his enthusiasm for a rare Costa Rican "barkbeater" pestle to his admiration for a dystopian anti-Soviet novel. He even went so far as to invent an Italian superlative for the word, "*bonjanglissima*," which invariably sends us into fits of giggles, even though few people will find the misapplication of my mother's unappetizing tastes in food to art and literature as screamingly funny as we do. The exclusivity of the joke is, of course, part of its appeal, for all friendships contain an element of misanthropy, a need to create a sharp distinction between Us and Them, an act of self-ghettoization through occult allusions that

enhances privacy, surrounding our intimacy with the linguistic equivalent of barbed wire.

My sense of humor changes dramatically when I am
with strangers. I become a hopeless victim of the Witty
Gay Man Syndrome, an affliction from which I have suffered ever since elementary school, when my principal
convened assemblies in the gymnasium to watch me staggering about on stage, playing a drunken woman in high
heels, or snarling at my exasperated neighbors in an imaginary movie theater, playing an imperious fashion plate
who stubbornly refused to remove her broad-brimmed
hat. To this day, whenever I am in the presence of straight
people, I often lapse into the tiresome antics of the rapier-
witted fop, more or less as if I were an African American
hamming it up as Little Black Sambo, or Prissy in *Gone
With the Wind* foolishly blubbering about Melanie's inop-
portune delivery. Like many other gay men, I obediently
perform the generic homosexual before heterosexual audiences, not because I am by nature an exhibitionist, but
because I grew up with an acute awareness of myself as the
butt of other people's jokes, an effeminate spectacle that
provoked embarrassed titters. There is only a thin line
between being a spectacle who is laughed at and a clown
who forces others to laugh with him. When gay men ham
it up before heterosexuals, demeaning themselves in the
role of court jesters, they are attempting to effect a political change in their audience, to alter its reaction from
mockery to amusement, and thus to transform themselves
from pathetic laughingstocks, who must endure the snick-

ers they inadvertently elicit, into zany wags who exert control over others through their deflating wisecracks. By means of comedy, the scapegoat turns the tables and exploits his ridiculousness as a new form of power, the power to reduce people to helpless giggles.

Most of my humor, however, is based less on wit than on slapstick distortions of my body. For instance, I use my disconcertingly malleable face, which stretches to positively equine lengths, in order to set my comic manner apart from the relatively expressionless solemnity of my appearance on the few occasions I choose to behave like an adult. This often abrupt change of costume is particularly important for a knee-slapping ham like me who insists on treading the fine line between humor and scorn and who therefore adopts an unequivocally facetious look to alert his victims that, when he tells them they are "complete fuck-ups," "uncultured savages," or "filthy little tramps who spread communicable diseases," he is pulling their leg.

Moreover, a simple fact of biology informs my entire sense of humor: I am at once effeminate and large and muscular. My conviction that my elegant sensibility is mismatched with my 190-pound frame, that body and soul have somehow gone irrevocably awry, has produced a major sight gag. Two grimaces stand out from my repertoire of scowls and pouts: the glamour puss of the Hollywood diva mugging for the camera and the mopey look of a wounded and defenseless child, his chin quivering, his lower lip bulging, his sad, saucer eyes welling with tears. Both routines rely on a form of three-dimensional collage in which I glue the face of a simpering beauty queen or a woebegone infant onto the body of a six-foot-two bruiser, a bizarre graft of anatomical non sequiturs that exaggerates the feeling of discomfort I experience with my body on a daily basis. Through these grotesque cut-and-paste juxtapositions of the dainty, hyperfeminine starlet and my hulking physique, I retell the joke that life has played on me, batting my eyes and making wistful references to my delicate constitution, my innocence, and my extreme youth ("I will be sixteen in February," I whisper when asked).

In addition to putting up with my compulsive face-making, friends and acquaintances must suffer through the ordeal of one of my most characteristic comic routines, a gag they know as "the Vulgar Dance." This hip-swiveling fandango is the mating ritual of my lewd alter ego, a voluptuous femme fatale who "lures men to their ruin" by "entangling them in a web of danger and intrigue," which I weave with hands that writhe like snakes, a protruding rear end that swishes back and forth until it virtually sweeps the floor, and a lazy tongue that slides lecherously over my moistened lips. I generously offer to teach these wanton moves to any onlookers who might want to hone their skills as temptresses, offering the testimonials of my many satisfied heterosexual customers—the ancient Hispanic doormen at my friend Jackie's, for instance, who I claim leap to their feet every time I enter her building, their decrepit voices crying out for me to dance.

Shimmying my shoulders and crossing my eyes as if I were experiencing convulsions of uncontrollable lasciviousness, I transform my awareness of being a monstrous curiosity, a raging middle-aged queen whom no straight man in his right mind would find attractive, into a source of amusement. The laughingstock uses his ridiculousness as the material of his shtick, making the very thing that repels his audience the cause of their attraction to him as a performer.

Being funny for me almost always involves a sex change into a celebrity, a bawdy act of cabaret drag, a performance that stems, not from any desire to be a woman, but from my emphatic decision to be a man, to costume myself in muscles, the real form of transvestism in my life. One actress in particular has had a profound effect on my sense of humor: Faye Dunaway imitating Joan Crawford in *Mommy Dearest*. My own imitation of Crawford consists largely of a single multipurpose facial expression, that of the thwarted megalomaniac, whom I impersonate by stretching back my lips, bugging out my eyes, and assuming a lockjaw expression of suppressed rage every time someone tells me that the meal I've prepared needs salt, that I've cranked up the air conditioning too high in the word processing center, or that it's my turn to take out the garbage. I frequently feign outrage at imaginary affronts to my dignity, unpardonable instances of lèse-majesté by plebeians who fail to treat me with the reverence I deserve, provocations I greet by turning my detractors into stone, dazzling them with the full force of my awe-inspiring countenance. When I was a child, I fantasized that I could control people with my eye beams, that I could frighten them simply by stabbing them with a gimlet look, the Medusa fantasy of a gay boy who felt physically powerless and who was mercilessly lampooned for his failure at sports. By casting basilisk glances inappropriately wherever I turn, I revisit this pipe dream of my youth and free myself from the caustic bitch who, with an incinerating glare, forces others to do her bidding. Imperiousness never succeeds in my comic world, no matter how intently I glower at the rabble, performing a running charade of the prima donna who imagines she has more power than she does and who must tolerate the insubordination of underlings who refuse to pay sufficient homage to her beauty.

My drag routines form an essential part of a lifelong campaign of self-deprecation in which I vilify myself as a "fat old fag"; point out to others that "there is a certain degree of masculinity in my femininity — but only a certain degree"; or laugh at the last time I took an airplane, having spent the trip next to a jock in a baseball cap who was somewhat taken aback by the sight of a fully grown man quaking in his seat beneath the winter coat he had thrown over his head, so stoned on Valium that "my shit could have been sold on the street as a controlled substance." The delight I take in knocking myself off my own pedestal is partly the result of internalizing the amused reactions of homophobic spectators who entertain themselves by whispering conspiratorially as I pass, giggling at my broad, overdemonstrative gestures and girlish, bow-legged waddle. It is as if I believed that by assuming their critical point of view and acknowledging my absurdity I will forestall their heckling. Only unwitting dupes can be ludicrous, never those who embrace their preposterousness and demonstrate that they are fully aware of sticking out like a sore thumb, a recognition that short-circuits ridicule, since the presumably witless stooge shows that he too is laughing, indeed, that he is the one making the joke at his own expense, not the home boy trying to impress his girlfriend by yelling at a fag on the streets. By constantly maligning myself, I do my critics' work for them and beat them to the punch line, thus depriving them of the satisfaction of being the comedian, the entertainer, since I myself have appropriated this privileged position.

As early as my late teens, self-deprecation became a kind of dare, a wager I made with myself, a game of chicken in which I sought to find out how much self-knowledge I could tolerate. In the course of writing my chapter on my gestures, for instance, I studied the way I moved by making a videotape of myself dancing naked to Sylvester's "Mighty Real," an obscene spectacle of a man with a dimpled ass bumping, grinding, and flapping his arms like a whale struggling unsuccessfully to get airborne. During a dinner party I hosted, I mentioned that the episode was "one of the most disgraceful events of my life" and then, throwing caution to the winds, decided to test my capacity to endure criticism and played the tape on the spot, much to the amusement of my guests, who naturally did not find the video as appalling as I did.

For many years, I have made it a practice to turn the most embarrassing things that happen to me into dinner conversation, to unmask myself in public situations, and expose to others the very incidents that frighten or demean me — gaffs, malapropisms, and insults that, were I to follow my instincts, I would never mention. Instead, I resist my impulse to hold my tongue and use things like the vitriolic comments my books receive ("total crapola," "obnoxious drivel," "a truly awful book") or such accidents as the time I farted while teaching as opportunities for laughter. For months after the publication of my last book, *Cute, Quaint, Hungry, and Romantic*, I joked among friends about its failure by varying its title every time I mentioned it: *Cute, Quaint, Ignored, and Remaindered* or *Crude, Cruddy, Crappy, and Crass*. Much as one makes bathing fun for children by turning it into a game, I make an uproarious postprandial pastime out of another form of hygiene, the cauterizing anguish of self-analysis.

A case in point is one of the most troubling skeletons in my closet, Little Fingers, a moth-eaten souvenir from my first long relationship, which ended over a decade ago. To our mutual chagrin, my former lover and I were obsessive baby-talkers and impersonated an entire cast of infantile characters, the major one being a spoiled brat who burbled and cooed while waving at others, as proof of her vulnerability, the stumps of her tiny fingers and toes. When we broke up, I suddenly realized that the dramatis personae of our love life had been silenced forever and even experienced a period of inconsolable mourning for this massacre of the innocents, this holocaust of phantasmal putti. Within the last few years, however, I have exhumed Little Fingers from the grave and now bring her out at parties where I perform in front of large groups routines I was, for good reason, once deeply ashamed of, wiggling at perfect strangers the mutilated digits of adorable thumbs and pinkies. I perform this act of corpse desecration on a former mascot of a failed love affair in order to consign her to her final resting place, to drive a stake through her heart so that she can never rise again as a harrowing reminder of past idiocies. By transforming shame into comedy, I at once triumph over experiences that remain disturbing if they are hidden and entertain other people, their laughter offering an incentive for further self-investigation. Humor is for me a method of comprehension, a way of experiencing pain intelligently well outside of the original mortifying context in which it occurred, of recalling events so traumatic that they induce a kind of amnesia that dooms us to repeat our mistakes unless we can create a safe environment in which to study them.

Although I am convinced of the power of self-deprecation to face my fears, as well as to enhance my appeal to others through a type of unilateral disarmament, I am fully aware that my modesty may just be *amour-propre* in disguise. There is, for instance, the pride I take in what Koestler called "wallowing," in showing off my courage, in flaunting my fallibility and proving to others that nothing is too degrading to escape my candor, that I am impregnable to shame and will divulge my most compromising secrets before large audiences or even publish them, as I do here, in a book. What's more, habitual self-deprecation often depends on the presumption that one's audience really cares about one's own put-downs, indeed, that it is even aware that an act of deflation has occurred, as in the case of my nude dance, which *I* perceived as a terrible loss of face but which left my friends indifferent, unaware that some fifteen extra pounds of flabby butt cheeks were jiggling to that driving beat. The hilarity of boasting of one's ugliness, incompetence, and effeminacy grows out of an exaggerated sense of one's importance, for it is difficult to belittle that which others already find insignificant, whose value is apparent only to the person who insists on discrediting character traits or physical abnormalities that are of consequence to no one.

Before the twentieth century, parents instilled in their children the importance of sobriety, even staidness, which kept them from succumbing to the follies of irreligious levity. A key part of my own moral education, by contrast, was what my parents referred to again and again as "a sense of humor," a willingness to laugh at oneself, to roll with the punches, and even to allow others to take occasional potshots at one's dignity. At some point in elementary school, a teacher who had lost control of his students in a blizzard of spitballs and paper airplanes kept me after class and asked me, as the goody-two-shoes of the group, what I thought he was doing wrong. I smugly repeated the lesson my parents had taught me and told him that the problem was that he had no sense of humor, a failing he tried diligently to overcome during the next few months by flashing a winning rictus at his terrified pupils and issuing joyless chortles of unconvincing glee. Being without a sense of humor was, for me, like being without a limb, a deformity of character caused by the belief that you were untouchable, better than others, holier-than-thou, elevated over the common man. The willingness to laugh often and laugh loud is nothing short of a political mandate in a democracy, a way of leveling imbalances of power by subjecting both the billionaire and the low man on the totem pole to the same egalitarian spirit of irreverence. By inculcating in me the necessity of maintaining a sense of humor, my parents were teaching me how to carry myself in a society ostensibly intolerant of class differences, laughter being the great solvent of inequalities and a way of ensuring that no one ever mistook me for being stuck-up and standoffish, a prig who refused to drop his reserve for the sake of a good joke, often at his own expense.

My education in humor was, however, out of line with my experience as a homosexual, the ultimate butt of popular laughter. At the same time that I was taught that I must submit to the teasing of my friends, I increasingly found myself in situations in which I could not laugh, in which I felt isolated, and in which irreconcilable differences emerged between the prejudices of guffawing homophobes and the snobbish sensibility of a beleaguered aesthete who formulated his sardonic and skeptical sense of humor in response to the taunts of the ill-mannered moral majority. Once during graduate school, I was working out in the weight room when a student began reviling "dykes and fags who have no sense of humor," a statement premised on the paradoxical idea that, to have a sense of humor, the homosexual must willingly participate in his own defamation. I snuck up behind him and said, "That's right, we have no sense of humor whatsoever," whereupon we became embroiled in a knock-down-drag-out in which, for nearly thirty minutes, we argued heatedly about homosexuality before dozens of bewildered jocks, their eyes fixed on us in disbelief. My parents may have taught me the necessity of using humor to prove that I was no different from anyone else, but it is difficult for the escaped slave to fraternize companionably with the posse hot on his trail. As a result, I have grown to dislike popular humor, which frequently brings to mind the glee of a lynch mob and arouses in me fears of being tarred and feathered by the two thirds of Americans who still think that homosexuality is an illness. Because of this, I have always detested zany comedies and find sitting in an audience of people hyperventilating over a panty raid, a beer-chugging contest, or a cafeteria food fight a profoundly alienating experience, one that brings out in me the misanthrope who rejects his egalitarian upbringing and embraces an elitism that has been thrust upon me by the intolerance and cruelty of the lowest common denominator. My sense of humor is the product of two contradictory forces, my liberalism and my elitism, the leftist tendencies of parents who sought conscientiously to rid me of contempt for my fellow man and my fellow man's unwillingness to return the favor. I have therefore developed two distinct senses of humor, self-deprecation, which I use to prove that I am like everyone else, a poor schmuck who frequently falls flat on his face, and satire, which I use to exact revenge on a society that has made me pay a high price for my eccentricities.

And yet while I find it difficult to establish any common ground with the masses, I find it just as difficult to feel any sympathy for the self-appointed police force that is now patrolling the public realm for verbal hate crimes against minorities. I recoil at once from the intolerance of the hoi polloi and the righteousness of the politically correct, which has inadvertently created a new form of cabinet humor that has entirely displaced the dirty joke: ethnic humor, the racial slurs that we bandy back and forth in private, cackling over such classic examples of closeted urban racism as "How many African Americans does it take to change a light bulb? Two, one to hold the bulb and the other to drive the Cadillac in tight circles." I will never be able to hold public office because I make off-color jokes, not only about blacks, but about Asians, Russians, Jews, the handicapped, the obese, women, and, most important of all, homosexuals, a group with whom, appearances to the contrary, I share only superficial affinities. Writing to thank a friend who, in the early 1980s, lent me her apartment on a drug-infested street where the black dope dealers swiftly converged on me whenever I dashed for her front door, I told her that I kept them at bay by brandishing my fist triumphantly in the air and yelling, "Free Nelson Mandela!" and "Darkies are people too!" A culture of euphemists has created an underground of remorseful dysphemists who, the minute the coast is clear, are afflicted with Tourette's syndrome, with an insane desire to desecrate sacred taboos.

I was raised to believe that humor destroyed hierarchies of power and brought everyone down to the same level playing field, but I clearly do not believe this, as became all too evident one day at work when, bored out of my mind on an especially tedious Sunday, I scrambled up on top of my desk and led the entire room in a rousing rendition of "Climb Every Mountain." In the middle of my performance, an important partner brought in a job, whereupon I immediately stopped and sheepishly crawled back down, even though he was clearly amused by my outrageous skit. I torment my coworkers by commenting on their philandering husbands and the recuperative month they spent, although supposedly hiking in the Rockies, actually strapped to a gurney in the Betty Ford clinic, but the minute a lawyer enters the room, I become mature, accommodating, and professional, as sedate and self-effacing as a British butler. One does not "tickle" those who occupy a higher social station; they are the ones who "tickle" us. I can direct my mock insults only to my equals and inferiors, never to my betters, a sad testament to the caste-bound nature of my humor, which is extraordinarily circumspect about whom it chooses as the butt of its satire. Only those in power have the right to initiate laughter, whereas their staff must behave like profession- al claqueurs, an audience of bashful lackeys reduced to stitches by the boss's bon mots. Applauding is an expres- sion of submission; laughing, the homage the weak pay to the strong.

One of the reasons that I often resist the seductions of collective laughter, aside from the fact that all too often I am its target, is that, around the age of thirteen, I began to define myself through a deeply antisocial act of self-asser- tion: the refusal to laugh, specifically, to laugh with my two sisters. Even now, I feel embarrassed about our orgies of uncontrollable hilarity, joyless binges of cruel laughter in which we violated each other's physical privacy, pinched each other's asses, slipped our hands down each other's pants, and groped each other's breasts and crotch- es. We attempted to outdo each other in our obscenities, referring to Mother's vagina as "From Whence We Came" and tackling each other in pretend rape scenes in which we mumbled over and over again, as we humped and fon- dled, "You're so tight, so good; God, you're good." These mirthless laugh-a-thons may have been simply an expres- sion of cabin fever, the hysteria of a completely atomized American family that, because we moved so often, never managed to establish roots in any community and thus had no public existence, no one to keep us in line, no wit- nesses to check our bad behavior, a duty that our parents relinquished as their own problems began to absorb more and more of their attention. Leading an insular existence, we lost all sense of ourselves as individuals and became one amorphous entity with no clear boundaries between us. Exhausted by my complete loss of privacy and by the erosion of my autonomy, I finally started to resist the force of this ritual, which, even now, thirty years later, emerges whenever we get together, the old habits rising from the depths, as if nothing whatsoever had intervened, as if we had just left the room and returned only a second later to find that we were still the children of an unhappy couple trapped on a cul-de-sac in a decaying Southern town. Growing up for me meant becoming more serious, more dignified, more solemn, capable of deciding when *not* to laugh and of mapping out the limits of my sense of humor, where *I* began and my sisters ended, erecting a fire wall between Me and Them, a barrier essential to the formation of my identity.

The enervation I experienced on a small scale during these perverse family frolics, I experience on a large scale with society as a whole, with a culture that suffers from too much laughter, from humor overload, from living in the shadow of mass entertainment. The barrage of throw-away one-liners that are tossed off at ten-second intervals on sitcoms reappear in an infinitely less clever and scripted guise in our own conversations, which copy episodes from *Friends* and *Sabrina*. Since we are now all comedians, who laugh between one hundred and four hundred times a day, humor, not courtesy, is our primary social skill. Much as cats meow and dogs bark, mankind uses laughter as its own characteristic type of animal cry, a bird call, or, as one neuroscientist has put it, "an aesthetically and sonically impoverished 'human song.'" Turkeys gobble, lizards engage in group head-bobbing, and human beings laugh as part of a behavioral chain reaction, with our staccato bursts functioning as a roll call of the tribe, a way of signaling that "I am on this branch here, I am on this telephone wire, I am perched to your right on the fence." Such a social reflex is easily exploited by the forces of commercialism, by television, film, and advertisements, all of which attempt to disarm our ability to think by reducing us to mindless laugh tracks. This extortion naturally induces not only fatigue with our spasmodic gobbling but intense resentment, which makes people like me long to wipe the smiles off our faces and adopt a stance of grief-stricken solemnity, to secede from the pack, much as I seceded from the peer group of my siblings in order to preserve some semblance of self-respect.

5

Fucking

Once when I was six or seven, I was caught red-handed playing doctor with a neighborhood boy. We had draped my ugly brown bedspread decorated with lassos, cowboy boots, and ten-gallon hats over the edge of my trundle bed so that its lower level became a cozy, if cramped, cabin, when my sister Lynn barged into the room and stuck her head into my imaginary consultation booth just as I was about to plunge an invisible hypodermic needle into Tony Smith's naked buttocks. Her raucous laughter rang out through the entire house and she fled down the hallway screaming, "I caught them, I caught them playing doctor" while I flew after her in hot pursuit, slipping and sliding on the waxed wood floors, begging her not to expose me, to utter my shameful secret in her shrill, satirical voice. My parents were entertaining and she burst in among their astonished guests (Tony's wide-eyed mother and father among them) and blurted out what she had seen, oblivious to my sobbing pleas and my helpless, sputtering howls, "I hate you, I hate you, I hope you die." I do not remember whether I was punished; but since ours was a civilized household, I think it more likely that Lynn was scolded for being a tattletale and my medical ventures were never mentioned again, left to fester in my parents' memories along with mounting evidence of my aberrant sexual development.

Over twenty years later, I was caught again, this time in a notorious cruise park in Cambridge, Massachusetts, the Bird Sanctuary, a secluded wildlife refuge frequented mainly by joggers and the cops, who made a sport of harassing the legions of gay men who had sex in trampled clearings and densely foliaged bushes. I had removed every stitch of clothing except for my high-top Converse sneakers and was masturbating a distinguished gentleman in a three-piece suit when I heard a rhythmical slapping sound, the menacing whack of two night sticks striking the palms of two scowling men in blue who proceeded to escort us to their cruiser and write out citations for public sex. I was speechless with rage and humiliation and could barely suppress my urge to implore them not to tell, to betray my shameful secret, as I had entreated Lynn some twenty years before, her mocking laughter taunting me as cruelly as the officiousness of these two civic vigilantes, so smugly confident of the justice of their gratuitous brutality. Hours later, I marched into the offices of the

Cambridge Human Rights Commission in order to lodge a complaint against the police department, no longer a blubbering child pleading for compassion from his sister but an emancipated gay man who had found the courage to strike back.

Although it was useful to me personally to express my anger by lodging this ultimately pointless grievance, there was something politically disingenuous about my fury at being caught by the police, who surely had better things to do with the taxpayers' money than ensnare harmless poofs wanking off in the woods. Would I have even gone to the Bird Sanctuary if I had known it wasn't crawling with cops famous for the pleasure they took in humiliating queers, if the excitement of sex out-of-doors wasn't accompanied by the titillating thrill of a gamble, the hazard I ran defying the odds right beneath the noses of the vice squad? In fact, I contacted the Human Rights Commission to complain about the very thing I still find most exciting about sex: the chance of being discovered. It is not as if I am by nature an exhibitionist, but simply that, since childhood, I have by necessity had some of my most intense sexual experiences in situations jeopardized by the possibility of imminent exposure and therefore have become addicted to the aphrodisiac of stealth, which, virtually by accident, has been incorporated into my psychology of arousal.

Like most children, I had few opportunities for privacy while growing up and could have sex only by evading the meddling supervision of prying adults who did everything in their power to keep their offspring underfoot, forcing me to make my first tentative erotic experiments in public places: in the woods, where I engaged in circle jerks with randy schoolmates; in the tents of backyard campouts, where I played strip poker with my friends; and in the lofts of barns, where I discovered the pleasures of "horsey" while straddling bales of hay. Even today I am constantly looking for public places that would "work" for sex, half-concealed alcoves in subway stations, open janitor's closets in office buildings, and blind corners in shopping malls, locations in which I can recreate the original conditions of my earliest experiences. With no locks on our bedroom doors, I once masturbated with my friends in an atmosphere of unnerving suspense, a world in which we lay in bed at slumber parties waiting on tenterhooks for our parents to go to sleep and in which we felt each other up in refrigerator boxes and the makeshift forts we built in empty lots. After decades of hiding to make love, guiltily stealing away into the woods and into cavernous culverts at the outskirts of town, I now recognize my snooping sister as the muse of my sex life, permanently stationed at the keyhole where her spying eyes heighten the secrecy of my encounters.

It is in part because of my need for surreptitiousness that I am so fascinated by sex with straight men. Having come out of the closet at the age of thirteen, participated in the gay rights movement, and written extensively about my homosexuality for general interest publications, I cannot credibly sustain the fiction that I am ashamed of my sexual preferences, even though gay men like me long nostalgically to recreate the sense of the forbidden that, before they came out, increased the covert pleasures of their dark, furtive gropings. I therefore relive my irrecoverably diminished sense of this illicitness by seeking out heterosexual men, who are still uncomfortable with the impermissibility of their secret excursions into an outlaw world that, after decades of familiarity, I find at best banal, pitifully free of taboos, so safe, so commonplace, that its most flagrant sexual outrages are incapable of bringing even a blush to my cheeks. I feed on the anxiety of sex-starved straights, on their mortifying shame, which I enjoy secondhand, astonished, even delighted, by credulous tricks, scared out of their wits, who ask me in all seriousness if there are any hidden surveillance cameras in the room and whether I will promise not to tell their wives and employers.

I am in part obsessed with straight men because, on some visceral level immune to the dictates of common sense, I still believe that they are more authentically male than I am, that they are the Real McCoy whereas I am an emasculated eunuch who must grovel before their superior strength and virility. As difficult as it is to admit in the present political climate, every time I give head to a straight man I throw my emancipation out the window and roll back decades of gay liberation, reverting to a pastoral world of oppression, a make-believe oasis of prejudices where I indulge in a miniature gay bashing. In the presence of heterosexuals, I reenact my degradation before my white masters whom I long to wait on hand and foot, to prove to them the full extent of my subservience and to punish myself for my weakness and effeminacy, for my failure to learn how to dribble a basketball in gym class and for my pronounced wiggle, which to this day elicits catcalls from rednecks in passing cars.

I was not always interested in heterosexuals and am not even certain that, before the onset of puberty, I recognized any differences between the gay boys and the straight ones — between Jim Powers, a swaggering Lothario who flirted shamelessly with the girls in our elementary school, and Tim Stringer, my lover of several years, a goonish gay blade with a bulbous nose and an enormous prick with whom I staged episodes of *Queen for a Day.* By the age of twelve, I had seduced virtually all of the boys in the neighborhood by playing a game we called "wife," a pretext for furious sessions of frottage in which I invariably lay naked on my back with my heels in the air while my "husband" thrust and heaved above me. In fact, of the fifteen or twenty boys who lived near me, only one managed to wriggle out of my clutches, my best friend, Steve, a studious redhead who disapproved strongly of my escapades and loathed my involvement with Tim, who forced me to participate in such stunts as climbing up in a tree and, in a husky, feminine voice, calling out to passing college students, "Hello there, young man." Steve and I came to blows over Tim when he asked me one day why I was hanging out with that "sissy" and whether I too was a "homo." In a significantly girlish move, I slapped him hard across the face and yanked his hair during a fight that marked a symbolic break with the straight world and a new allegiance with my gay peers, whom my schoolmates disliked, troubled by my tittering intimacy with Tim and his minion, Nick, as well as by the female impersonations that I staged at school assemblies, riotous skits that pro-. voked in Steve such acute embarrassment that he approached me after one performance and exclaimed, "I wouldn't have been caught dead doing what you did up there."

By the time I was thirteen, I was identifiably gay, and I would never again move as freely among my "husbands," who unaccountably ostracized me the moment I acquired gay friends and gay mannerisms. My desire for hetero-sexuals can be traced back to this rupture, to my dawning realization that the gate had shut, the key had turned, and that I was locked out forever, having become a "fem" who compromised the masculinity of my former compatriots. Only when I was shunned by straight boys did I begin to desire them over my more accessible gay friends, only when they were unwilling to be seen with me, when I emerged as a recognizable queer, a faggot who collapsed into conspiratorial giggles with his "girlfriends"; abhorred the mildewed smells of the gymnasium; and sat entranced in his mother's rocker belting out songs from his favorite album, *The Sound of Music*. Desiring straight men is not only an act of self-loathing but a rapprochement, a reunion with old lovers, an attempt to overcome an ancient estrangement and reenter that polymorphous world in which there were no distinctions between straight and gay boys, distinctions that were thrust upon me as my desire for men acquired a social, behavioral dimension.

My sudden, inexplicable divorce from my seraglio of "husbands" had an unforeseen consequence: an underwear fetish that I enjoy even now. One of the most embarrassing incidents from my early adolescence occurred at a tea party held for faculty wives where I cornered the hostess's chatty, five-year-old daughter and demanded that she lead me to her beguilingly handsome, teenage brother's underwear drawer. She promptly scurried off into the room where the coffee klatch was exchanging ladylike pleasantries and nibbling packaged cookies and asked her deeply religious mother, as if she were asking for permission to play on the swing set, "CAN I SHOW DANIEL BOB'S UNDERWEAR DRAWER?" Trauma has erased all memory of the shock with which this question must have been received. Although I have never again been so indiscreet, I have long had to settle for gleaming white briefs in the absence of the straight man who wears them, mainly because his shorts are so much more tractable than he is, so much more tolerant, quite willing to allow me to fondle them without risking a potentially violent rebuff. My interest in underwear escalated into a full-blown obsession as the rift separating me from the straight world widened. Fetishes are synecdochic pastimes in which the part stands for the whole—idolatrous attachments that signify lack, unfullfilment, the inability to obtain the real thing and the necessity of making do with a substitute, a fragrant undergarment incapable of shouting homophobic epithets or punching me on the jaw.

Jockey shorts also last far longer than love affairs. I have never in my life been able to maintain a sexual relationship for more than a few dates, after which a paralyzing marital apathy sets in or, as one gorgeous fem dyke I know calls it, "lesbian bed death." I was taught that homosexuality is bad and dirty and illicit, the subversive activity of leering profligates who skulk around playgrounds and haunt subway bathrooms, and the minute sex becomes wholesome, a sanctioned relationship with all of the connubial trappings—a mother-in-law, a favorite restaurant, a dog held in joint custody—I lose interest, my all-consuming need for shame thwarted by a surfeit of approval.

And herein lies my dilemma. It is as impossible to have faith in the forbidden in a world of total permissiveness as to have faith in God after Nietzsche and the atom bomb. I am a typical instance of the conflict of theory and practice. There is a major disjunction between my political awareness as an enlightened gay man, who cannot by any stretch of the imagination believe that gay sex is wrong, and my reactionary libido, which seeks to recreate the guilt and shame of my childhood and turn every butt-fuck and blow job into a lynching in which I live out increasingly untenable fantasies of being a low-down pervert who needs to be punished for unspeakable longings that have become perfectly admissible. What's more, gay liberation has complicated matters even further by forbidding us to play into the hands of the right wing and mention the fact that, for many homosexuals, shame is still integral to desire, a fact that appalls the politically correct, who insist that gay sex is a well-adjusted and life-affirming expression of an interpersonal commitment. As a consequence, we not only feel guilty because society tells us that we are disgraceful pariahs, but we also feel guilty because we enjoy *being* disgraceful pariahs when our leaders assert that we must categorically deny our stigma and embrace our wholesomeness in a spirit of "pride," the dignity and self-respect that casts a pall over the recreational activities of those of us who prefer, at least in the bedroom, to remain in a state of disrepute. Gay liberation has ironically increased the dishonor we feel about our sexual preferences, teaching us to suppress the truth lest we provide fodder for our opponents' prejudices. Under these conditions, is it any wonder that the men I trick with seldom satisfy me more than once before the precarious illusion of the clandestine is shattered by my increasing knowledge of their lives, interests, and professions?

Theory has had at least one direct effect on practice — namely, on the manner in which I cruise. I do not look askance at the men who attract me, casting shamefaced glances in their direction, lowering my eyes modestly and then sneaking another peek, but instead stare at them brazenly and even spin around 180 degrees to ogle their butts as they saunter past, just as packs of horny construction workers gawk at pretty women forced to run the gauntlet during their lunch hours. Gay liberation has taught me to express my desires openly, to dispense with the shifty game of peekaboo with which most gay men cruise, concerned as they are not only with being caught and assaulted with the insult "What are you looking at, faggot?," but also with lowering their value in the eyes of other homosexuals, who seek to preserve the excitement of secrecy, of the nocturnal prowl, which lends an air of underhanded mystery to the search for sex. Intolerant of such charades, I look men full in the face and examine their bodies from head to toe, lingering over the bulge in their crotches in order to make it clear to those who might be intimidated by my height and deceptively manly physique where my true interests lie. My libido is an odd mixture of flagrancy and stealth, shameless glad-to-be-gay self-assertion and closeted dissembling, political sophistication and regressive yearning to restore the pornographic dimension of behavior that has become as routine to me as breathing.

Another reason that I cannot maintain sexual interest in anyone for any length of time is that I am a remarkably unsensual person whose attitude toward sex is aridly intellectual and who is strangely unaroused by gentle caresses, preferring instead to be manhandled by selfish beasts, not grazed by fluttering fingertips. Fucking for me revolves around a rigidly defined ritual based on the allegory of domination and submission. Ever since I adopted my role of "wife" in childhood and strapped my legs around the thrusting pelvis of my diminutive "husband," I have made love for only one reason, for the euphoric experience of being used, an imaginary act of emasculation so all-consuming that my physical responses are nothing more than irrelevant by-products of a mental event. Detached from the senses, such highly conceptual sex cannot occur with the same partner more than once, not just because repeated encounters automatically legitimize what is meant to be illicit, but because the fiction of control is by definition short-lived. The minute one learns that the "top" collects stuffed animals, sings in the Gay Men's Chorus, and knows all of the words to *Funny Girl*, he emerges in all of his comic fallibility. Tops can preserve the tenuous illusion of their omnipotence and bottoms the even more perishable illusion of their fragility and defenselessness only when they remain empty ciphers, perfect strangers to one another — a pretense that lasts for fifteen to forty-five minutes, after which the postcoital tête-à-tête inevitably produces a rude romantic awakening.

What's more, the game of domination and submission is unsupported by the realities of current social conditions and is dramatically out of synch with a prosperous democracy in which real power is not exemplified by the muscles of the brawny action hero but by the calculators and cell phones of the businessman, the flabby, middle-aged executive who can send the Dow into a tailspin simply by faxing a spreadsheet or announcing a layoff or merger. In the bedroom, I enter a time machine and travel back to a different social order, an archaic society in which brute strength, not venture-capitalist cunning, was the means of achieving supremacy. This type of domination no longer serves any purpose but we persist in admiring it long after physical dexterity has come to be valued solely out on the basketball court and the football field. The libido has an ancient memory and has not caught up with modern times. Existing in an artificial realm that bears no relation to how we experience power in the real world, the ephemeral drama of master and slave cannot survive outside the theater of the bedroom. We are therefore driven to replace our leading men at every performance in an effort to shore up such an untenable fiction.

The pretense of submission is particularly assailable because I am so effeminate. I turn gay men off not only because I am "spottable," marked by the disfiguring brand of the subculture, but because I have adopted a posture of sustained irony, the very essence of camp. This archness negates the boyish innocence many people require to intensify the debauchery of gay sex and has no place within the context of a sacred ritual based on the conspiratorial earnestness of those who would like to believe that they belong to an underground cabal. Only the guilt-free can afford the luxury of laughing during sex, cracking jokes that are incongruous, even tasteless, in a situation that depends on the illusion that we are transgressing taboos. Humor requires a degree of relaxation, of guiltlessness, a disrespectful lack of gravity for men who prefer to make love like morticians in poker-faced silence, intolerant of unseemly levity, grimly committed to the serious business of being unwholesome and breaking the law.

Given the theoretical nature of my sex life and my knowledge that both my own passivity and my partner's control of me are a charade, it is surprising how intolerant I am of S/M, how I loathe props like dildos, riding crops, and harnesses, and how I scoff at the typical pornographic scenes with which lovers entertain themselves, acting out such plots as the convict and the prison guard or the frat brother and his rush-week pledge. Although I admit that my own submission to another man is little more than a put-on, the pot insists on calling the kettle black and holds in contempt those who take the allegory too seriously, who wield cat-o'-nine-tails, wear buttless leather chaps, and attend slave auctions for charitable causes like Toys-for-Tots. Perhaps S/M represents for me the *reductio ad absurdum* of my own fantasies, whose histrionics I can conceal from myself only if the plot is handled with a high degree of tact, without all of the fanfare that reveals too clearly the hokum of this psychological scenario, which cannot withstand the close scrutiny of the savage drama critic I become in the presence of amateur theatricals staged in makeshift dungeons equipped with stocks, slings, and whipping posts.

I also cannot make love to the same person because very early in my life I consciously disentangled sex from intimacy in a self-protective move that freed me from cloying romantic tendencies that once threatened to transform me into a serial obsessionist. At the age of sixteen, when I first had sex with an adult male, I had not yet separated fucking and romance. After a single disastrous romp with a local radio personality, I would escape to the family automobile where I would sit in a hormonal trance listening to the rich baritone of the man who had taken my virginity and then jilted me, leaving me alone in a stuffy car sticking to the hot plastic upholstery and hanging on every word he uttered about Brahms and Debussy. By the age of twenty-one, I had been obsessed with no less than four men (three of them straight) and deliberately set out to eradicate my sentimental fantasies by becoming what one gay writer has called "a big, fat, drunk, sloppy pass-around party bottom." Promiscuity enabled me to see sex in all of its crude biological insignificance, which I came to understand by ingesting enormous quantities of semen and allowing myself to be gang-banged against the trunks of trees in cruise parks, thereby divesting intercourse of its emotional baggage. Although I have loved two men very deeply since I adopted this unabashedly licentious stance as a tramp, my self-administered sex cure has worked miraculously and I have never again been obsessed with anyone. Heterosexuals often criticize gay men for severing sex and intimacy (an association that is, after all, very recent in human evolution), but when I consider the number of frustrated straight women whose lives have been derailed by quixotic fantasies about knights in shining armor, I am more than ever convinced of the psychological advantages of promiscuity for inuring oneself to the unimportance of sex.

Not only have I severed physical pleasure and intimacy but I have quarantined my erotic fantasies from the rest of my life so that they exert as minimal an effect as possible on my outlook and my relationships with my friends — indeed, with my lovers. Is there any conceivable way that my sexual practices reflect deep-seated personality traits? Am I looking for a daddy figure? Does my passivity in the bedroom spill over into the manner I adopt in my social interactions or into my attitude towards my writing? However strongly I am attracted to masculinity for purposes of sex, butch men are, quite simply, human dildos and usually bore me after fifteen minutes, so thoroughly do I detest being dominated in conversation, which I enjoy only when I succeed in establishing absolute parity, with each speaker taking turns and relinquishing the floor after talking for a reasonable length of time. In fact, I have designed my sex life to be as unlike my daily life as possible so that the reactionary impulses of my libido, my desire to submit to authority and my worship of fascist machismo, are safely contained in a recreational zone where they cannot affect behavior I consider altogether more important. Just as I began lifting weights so that I could be attractive without at the same time compromising my internal life and censoring my effeminacy, choosing instead to use my body as live bait for tricks, so I have protected myself from my dependent fantasies and my regressive worship of power by dividing myself into two separate creatures — a serious intellectual by day, a rutting bitch in heat by night. If the penalty for my divorce of sex and emotion is my complete incapacity to make love with anyone other than strangers, neglecting my connubial duties with my partners, it is a small price to pay for the psychologically hygienic act of creating a barrier between my daily life and self-abasing impulses that are stubbornly resistant to change, no matter how conscientiously I cultivate equal relationships outside the bedroom.

The sex lives of gay men are both enhanced and complicated by the fact that we are the ultimate consumerists of sex, of the disposable fuck. It is not a psychological impediment in gay men that prevents some of us from combining sex and intimacy but a dearth of opportunities among heterosexuals that makes them insist that intercourse should occur only within the context of emotional commitment, a point of view that grows out of deprivation, leading many people to fetishize every grope and French kiss because it costs such effort to secure acceptable partners. The homosexual's conspicuous consumption of sex does, however, produce unique frustrations, as seen in an image that has haunted my life ever since I first became a whore: the image of the labyrinth, which emerges every time I go to a park or a bathhouse, Dante-esque spaces that, after I have downed a few drinks, begin to seem like gigantic board games filled with cul-de-sacs and blind corridors. Cruising is a Piranesian experience in which I am forced to pace back and forth along the same paths, sidewalks, and hallways, squandering hours retracing my steps, taking the lefthand trail at the fork in the pavement and then doubling back to take the right only to end up where I started. The labyrinth structures my vision of the wastefully labor-intensive business of cruising and serves as an apt symbol of my sex life, which is at once blessed with infinite abundance and cursed with infinite paralysis, with the stress of irresolution that keeps me circling like a vulture around fresh roadkill. How much time I have lost waiting for the arrival of someone more muscular than the man lurking in the shadows by the bridge, who is in turn waiting for someone more handsome than the clone hovering by the drinking fountain, who is hoping to meet the man he made love to the night before! It is with keen remorse that I think back on the time I have frittered away in the labyrinth and look ahead, with a sickening sense of anticipatory loss, to the countless hours I will so irresponsibly forfeit there in the future.

Until four years ago, the labyrinth was always located outside my apartment, but it has suddenly and, with disastrous consequences, taken up residence right on my desk where my screen saver beckons me like the song of a siren, luring me into America Online's chat rooms, the ninth circle of hell for cyber whores like me. The computer icon that AOL uses to indicate that one's modem has made a successful connection is a schematic crowd of faceless figures waving happily at the user, welcoming him into the neighborly fold of the "community," an image full of sinister associations after the many sleepless nights I have spent "chatting," trying desperately to get laid as I numb the pain of the extreme boredom involved in cruising the Web with copious quantities of alcohol. There are now actually support groups for AOL addicts, and, to my shame, I must admit that I am an ideal candidate for the cultish and manipulative group therapy of these proselytizing twelve-steppers. I have had to take radical measures to prevent the disruption of my privacy and peace of mind by the sudden emergence of this bathhouse on my mouse pad. I have signed over my account to my boyfriend, created a new "screen name" (AOL allows each member a total of eight separate e-mail addresses), and then asked him to impose "parental restrictions" on my new subaccount, blocking me from consorting with other Brooklynites. As an Internet junkie, I am now, according to the grades of censoriousness that concerned parents can impose on their dirty-minded offspring, somewhere just under the age of thirteen, experiencing — at forty-three — an appropriately immature second childhood.

Despite its abundance, sex for me is so conceptual that I do not in fact make love but jerk off, as if the encounter were nothing more than a skin flick projected on an internal screen. On the verge of middle age, I remain an infantile onanist who cannot maintain an erection unless he plays with himself, a bad habit I acquired because, like most people, I have grown accustomed to only one method of arousal which tolerates little variation, much as women become addicted to their vibrators and are never again satisfied with the real thing. My own vibrator is my thumb and index finger which, as an unwelcome third party in an otherwise intimate encounter, are always lodged between my body and my partner's, preventing us from truly embracing, from achieving full contact, which I have not enjoyed since my days as a "wife."

My constantly masturbating hand is not the only impediment to fuller contact. I developed my notion of sex quite independent of my actual experiences of it and have allowed myself to be indoctrinated by the visual hyperboles of pornography, which have created a schematic, televisual type of lovemaking in which the bodies are pried widely apart in order to make room for the camera, a device that is, in its clumsy intrusiveness, the exact equivalent of my masturbating hand. My disinterest in full body contact is in part the result of watching pornographic films which, in order to display to best advantage the muscles of the cast members, permit their bodies to touch only at the point of penetration, the visual fulcrum around which straggling arms and legs must be carefully arranged to prevent overlap and optimize the conditions for viewing. Sex on the screen is not about the sensation of touch, which film cannot, after all, convey to the audience, but about vision, about showing off the lean, depilated physiques of splendid specimens who flex and pose, flaunting the significant accomplishments they have made at the gym. Actors in X-rated films are beauty contestants who strut their stuff during a televised pageant that showcases their six-pack abs and rock-hard bubble butts, not their skills in the art of lovemaking. Porn sex is sex for the eyes, not for the hands, and when I make love, I too am indifferent to the tactile experience of intercourse and seek to turn each encounter into a beautiful cinematic image, a lovely, framed picture of a living, breathing artwork, which must be kept at arm's length in order to be appreciated in all of its statuesque perfection.

The assimilation of the highly visual aesthetic of pornography into my own fantasies can be seen in the way I position my body when I am being fucked. One of my favorite spots for sex is before an enormous, built-in mirror in my living room where I bend over to show off my enticing hams, so carefully maintained through a grueling regimen of squats. During anal intercourse, I seek out the most photogenic angle from which to admire our copulating bodies, as if I were detached from the event and were looking on, watching rather than participating, recreating the screen of my television set in the reflection in the mirror where I replay one of Catalina's or Falcon's recent blockbusters.

It is because of my desire to step out of the action and return to my seat in the audience that I almost never have sex on my bed, which I avoid for positions that are almost always partially upright, either on my knees or on all fours, never supine, my neck craning uncomfortably over my heaving partner's shoulder. The unsupported weight of a man's body crushing me flat turns me off, obscuring the image of the act by excessive contact, blocking my sight lines. What's more, I detest making love in the dark and insist that the scene be illuminated with bright lights that reveal every dimple and bulge, a preference that shows how profoundly pornographic images structure my erotic experiences, as if I had never left the sofa but were watching two strangers making love, actors who are forced to adopt contorted poses under the glaring wattage of the cameraman's floodlights in order to accommodate the onlooker's uncompromisingly selfish viewpoint.

My indifference to sensation also emerges in my attitude towards my tits, which are strictly off-limits during sex. Tricks who twist my nipples like radio dials are often stunned by the ferocity with which I smack their pincer-like fingers and dislodge their mouths nursing at my udders in preposterous *Madonna lactans* scenes that, for days, leave my aching dugs chafed and sore. In the gym, I give my undivided attention to building up my pectoral muscles with bench presses, inclines, declines, and dips, but in the bedroom, these cherished appurtenances are meant to be seen, not touched, admired as cosmetic accessories that provide food for the eyes, not for razor-sharp teeth. The fact that the one part of my body I exercise most diligently to enhance my sexual attractiveness serves no practical function in sex—unlike, say, my butt—shows how obsessed I am with the visual dimension of lovemaking, how I see myself solely as a stage prop that contributes to the pornographic appearance of the scene.

For most people, lovers are, by definition, sex partners, but this is not the case with me. During my first long relationship, which lasted for over six years, I made love with my boyfriend fewer than ten times, and it has now been at least three years since I have had sex with my current partner. And yet despite the presumed tragedy of "lesbian bed death," I persist in seeing these men as my "lovers," in part because I am a victim of my society's contempt for the spinster, the old maid who is considered too frigid to maintain what is, according to the righteous chauvinism of the monogamist, a warm, mature, nurturing, marital relationship. To trivialize what I feel for my boyfriend because it is devoid of lust, however, is to denigrate the very intimacy—indeed, the passion—ostensibly felt by those who—out of deprivation, in my view—are desperate to keep the fires burning, to feign sexual interest long after the chill of familiarity has cast its first frost over the honeymoon bower. How many wonderful marriages are destroyed by those who insist on fighting the force of habit, who dread the inevitable diminution of erotic interest, and who labor under the misconception that a relationship without fucking is a doomed relationship, that those who neglect their duties in the sack always end up out on the curb? In fact, for someone whose attitude toward sex is as unsensual as mine, I experience with my lover the sensual pleasures I can never achieve with tricks, relishing the feel of his skin and hair, adoring his lips kissing my face. Eliminating sex, with its pathologies and confusions, from our relationship has allowed me to experience all of the things that sex is supposed to provide but that it hasn't for the better part of human history: intimacy, communication, and warmth.

6

Moving and Making Faces

If, as many physical anthropologists believe, the origin of man's gestures was mimicry of his prey, of woolly mammoths and saber-toothed tigers, my own gestures mimic another set of extinct species: the tear-stained beauty queen, her tiara askew, cradling her bouquet of roses and cheesing it up for the judges; Carol Merrill emerging from behind the curtain of door number 1, the tips of her fingers tracing the outlines of a self-defrosting Frigidaire; the lewd stripper gyrating her hips and twirling her rhinestone pasties; and the poolside bathing beauty wearing glamorous horn-rimmed sunglasses and a one-piece swimsuit, pointing her toes while lounging in her deck chair. My broadest gestures form an archive of anachronistic feminine pouts and poses, of kittenish stances, girlish flutterings of the hands, and sultry moues that I have incorporated into the way I camp, into the parodic mode I assume when I am being playful, when I am goofing around with my colleagues at the law firm or giggling with a group of close gay friends.

When I am engaging in a serious conversation, however, my gestures all but disappear. I become a sphinx, inscrutable, inert, slipping into a type of motionlessness caused by suppressing my effeminacy, by putting my inner queen in a straight jacket, keeping her under house arrest. I gesticulate dramatically only when I am trying to be funny, when I am engaging in slapstick performances in which, far from being my true self, I am actually disowning my gestures, telling my audience that these movements are not mine, that they are the coquettish eyelash battings and seductive shoulder shimmies of Hollywood actresses and would-be vamps from the 1950s. My mannerisms often consist of a series of rejections of myself, of recantations in which I abjure my effeminacy as the hilarious behavior of a chorus girl in a burlesque, a saucy tart in feathers and furs whom I bring out like a circus animal at dinner parties, a routine that functions as a form of gestural hygiene, a way of distancing myself from socially unacceptable mannerisms.

I am on my most intense gestural guard on the few occasions when I must woo potential sex partners, a moment in which gay men almost universally become stiff as statues, lowering their voices to manly baritones, standing ramrod straight, and holding their arms at their sides in an implausibly simian fashion. For those of us who suffer from the curse of effeminacy, sex appeal and movement of any sort are antithetical and seduction involves paralysis, a conscientious attempt to restrain the high-pitched bray of the nelly, to lock our wrists in order to keep them from flapping, and to strut like bow-legged cowboys.

My profound ambivalence toward my effeminacy also emerges in the uncomfortable closeness between gestures I consider elegant and those that I have incorporated into my comic shtick, such as a movement I have dubbed my "maiden" gesture, which involves pressing three fingers to my bosom like a neurasthenic Victorian virgin, a move I perform when I make fun of myself, feigning amazement at friends' innocent remarks. When placed in exactly the same manner against my temple, however, these three fingers are meant to look graceful, intellectual, and even slightly melancholy, part of a pose of anguished introspection, the contemplative pensiveness of a tormented Byronic figure. The distressingly thin line between movements I consider ridiculous and those I consider stylish shows how permeable the boundary between parody and seriousness is in the way I carry myself and how my strenuous efforts to quarantine my effeminacy in the prison of comedy is always unsuccessful.

If stillness is the stopgap solution to silencing the effeminate clamor of my body, I am never fully successful in suppressing one part of myself in particular: my hands, which are in constant motion, stroking my lips, tugging playfully on my earlobes, twisting the hairs of my goatee into sharp Fu Manchu tips, and wandering aimlessly, with a mind of their own, over every surface in their immediate vicinity. While I am usually anxious to show that I am deeply involved in a conversation, nod obsessively, and gaze sympathetically at troubled friends, my hands are like mischievous children playing at my side, completely oblivious to what is being said, now drawing patterns on a corduroy pillow on my sofa, now fiddling with a button on the cuff of my sleeve. As one of the most sensitive parts of our bodies, hands are second only to eyes in their ability to gather information about the world, recording so many sensations that it is only a slight exaggeration to call them our antennae, the mechanisms by which we orient ourselves in space and identify the things around us. Because their very purpose is to function as built-in search parties sent out to survey the lay of the land, I cannot simply stop them from their uncontrollable quest for sensory data. Freud believed that massaging our lips was evidence of a labial fixation, when in fact what we are really stimulating is our fingertips. We are the victims of a *digital* fixation, a strange desire to explore our environments with hands that act like tentacles foraging for knowledge.

In order to protect their offspring from their own curiosity, parents try fruitlessly to reverse evolutionary history by insisting that their children remain still at all times, that their wayward hands lie quietly folded in

their laps, that their squirming arms are kept obediently at their sides, and that their kicking feet, paddling
impishly in the air, are planted firmly on the floor. The
ideal of the motionless child sculpture, the willess
automaton in a freshly laundered pinafore, was instilled
in me in childhood by adults who formed my gestural
conscience by equating inactivity with good behavior,
barking out commands to "sit still" the moment my
hands succumbed to eons of neurological training and
began rummaging around in my surroundings.

The primal conflict that has developed between the
child sculpture and my nomadic fingers emerges in my
most distinctive bad habit, my nail biting, my cuticle
ripping, the way I pick at myself until I bleed. And yet
no sooner do I manage to flay off a plump cuticle or a
bright red paring of thumb than my hands become each
other's parents and wrestle each other down into my lap
where they remain grounded on their best behavior for
no more than a few seconds before they rise up in the air
again to continue peeling, prodding, and picking. My
lap is the doghouse where my hands are exiled for punishment, only to break out of solitary confinement and
throw themselves back into the fray. In this characteristic rhythm of self-gnawing followed by short-lived
moments of self-control, the well-behaved child sculpture squares off with my gestural id in a duel in which
the ultimatum to remain motionless inevitably collapses
before my fingers' need to escape the excessive supervision of the invisible parent still scolding me from my lap.

Self-fiddling is also one of the key ways I express dis-engagement and nonchalance, which is a curiously vio-lent and untranquil state for me. I am constantly disap-pearing behind a nervous blur of fumbling fingers. Whether I am shredding a napkin to ribbons, carefully scraping the label off of a beer bottle, or tying plastic swizzle sticks in knots, my hands are vandals that destroy everything in their path, from the paper clips I twist into corkscrews to the leaves I yank off trees as I walk, defoliating bushes and the twigs of young saplings, creating a trail of debris, the wreckage of my attempts to suggest that I am relaxed, uninvolved, and self-assured.

My hands return sheepishly to my lap when I am introduced to strangers, a self-conscious moment in which I carefully lock my fingers together in a gesture that is meant to say "I have put down my tools, my hands are idle, I am unoccupied and am giving you my undivided attention." I press my fingers into the shape of a steeple or squash them tightly under my thighs, not only to show that I am listening politely, that I am no longer working (which is why folding one's hands in the business world, as a sign of inactivity — the opposite of diligence — is the highest compliment one can pay to a colleague) but also in tense public situations like sitting on a subway or standing in a crowded elevator, my eyes locked straight ahead, my hands crossed defensively in front of my crotch. In situations in which I feel uncom-fortable or detect even the slightest element of threat, all unnecessary motion ceases, I lower my head, and, like a forest animal paralyzed by the distant howl of a wolf, I resort to a form of primordial camouflage: motionlessness. When we are ill at ease, as is the case when we take public transportation and are thrown into potentially volatile situations with drunks, panhandlers, and screaming teenagers, our antennae retract, the agitated internal dialogue of our roaming hands abruptly ends, and we become as still as possible in an effort to avoid attracting the attention of potential predators. We withdraw into a dreamy solipsistic state in which we fool our attackers by blending into the vegetation, into the advertisements and the graffiti, convinced that, by assuming a catatonic pose, we have become invisible.

My fear of my effeminacy, as well as of other people, is only one of the reasons I keep my hands on a tight leash during serious conversations. I am also so restrained in my movements because I refuse to gossip and therefore seldom reenact past conversations. I maintain instead a high level of abstraction that precludes the very possibility of mimicry, the spontaneous caricaturing of one's cast of characters whose aggravating presence we evoke by means of angry stabs at one's chest, which indicate a rude remark, followed by a jab in the direction of an absent speaker to indicate an equally vicious retort. This obsessive pointing from one's own body to that of an imaginary foe are the speech tags of gripe sessions that consist largely of such statements as "So he says to me" and "So I says to her," a type of homespun theater in which one impersonates the pedestrian villains of one's day. Partly because I know full well how dull people find such self-congratulating routines and partly because, since I am a writer, very little happens to me that is worth reporting to others, my conversation tends to be by nature cerebral and my hands are like actors deprived of a script, Pirandello characters in search of a play, unable to accompany my speech and therefore abandoned to their own devices, nervously clawing each other to pieces in order to occupy themselves during moments in which most people rehash arguments with their bosses and coworkers.

Although I seldom "talk" with my hands, my typically abstract language fails me at significant moments when I automatically resort to miming gestures, especially when I am trying to delineate for people the characteristics of objects—their shape, length, height, weight, and width, as well as the distance that separates them—qualities I express by turning my hands into measuring sticks and my palms into the pans of scales that rise and fall. Before spoken language developed some 500,000 to 200,000 years ago, human beings probably communicated with each other by means of signs, through finger-pointing and fist-shaking, a crude vocabulary devoid of abstract concepts but useful for indicating such directions as left, right, up, down, over, and through, spatial information that remains to this day only partially expressible in words. The minute I need to describe the shape of a long-necked tribal fetish in the Metropolitan Museum or the terrain of a landscape, I resort instinctively to mimicry, sculpting in the air elongated cultic heads from New Guinea by pulling apart my hands, as if I were stretching taffy, and capturing the look of mountainous topography by moving them like a wave in order to suggest the undulation of hills. When the subject of my conversation becomes concrete, when it is about the objects of the physical world, I revert to an ancient gestural language created for the least conceptual kind of communication, a language intended for pure spatial navigation, for fording streams and finding shelter from the elements.

The fact that this language has been demoted into an anachronistic collection of gestural fossils can be seen in the disappearance of one of its key components: pointing, an act that is now considered impolite and is subject to swift parental correction, like burping or picking one's nose in public. Along with "please" and "thank you," I learned the pointing taboo in childhood and was sternly reprimanded for gaping, hand outstretched, at the fascinating deformities of misshapen passersby whose feelings, I was taught, could be wounded simply by my pointing at them, a seemingly magical act that could strip them of their selfhood and turn them into inanimate objects. Perhaps at one time we pointed at things we intended to kill and certainly we still point at people we intend to incriminate, using a gesture that has an almost shamanistic capacity to freeze a living being in its tracks and turn it into a motionless prisoner of our

– 117 –

accusations. The rise of the pointing taboo represents one of the most basic emendations of our early gestural vocabulary, a change that reflects our culture's increasing awareness of the subjectivity of others and the growth of a habit of empathy that our earliest ancestors probably had not yet developed.

Oddly enough, the pointing taboo is suspended in regard to my own body. I point at myself constantly, rudely, emphatically, particularly at my face, where both my dimple and my chin function as permanent sockets for my index finger. This curious act of self-objectification may simply be a way of alerting others to my presence, of saying "I am here, take notice of me," directing people's eyes to my inimitable countenance by means of a deliberate infraction of an important taboo. Self-pointing encourages others to engage in the boorish behavior we were taught to avoid as children, that of ogling someone as an entertaining spectacle — a faux pas that, despite our upbringing, we actually desire others to perform in relation to ourselves, preferring to be the center of attention rather than altogether ignored.

When my hand is not pointing at my cheek, it is usually holding a coffee cup or a pen, two props I find essential for gesturing. Quite aside from the fact that I drink a lot of coffee and write a lot of prose, cups and pens are stylistic prerequisites for me because they are faux cigarettes, as addictive as nicotine, gestural aids that I adopted after falling under the spell of Hollywood and the seductive image of the classic vamp exhaling plumes of blue smoke, the picture of composure as she tells her lover that she has just murdered her husband or blackmailed her boss. When I settle back into my recliner, bend my elbow, and raise my pen triumphantly in the air, flipping back my hand in order to expose the soft skin of my wrist, I am not only a pretend smoker, I am a pretend *female* smoker, and, what's more, a pretend wicked, naughty, and somewhat louche female smoker, a literary Jezebel whose unladylike habit suggests disdain for conventional morality. The Salems and Lucky Strikes of the Hollywood demimondaine — of Bette Davis in *All About Eve* and Barbara Stanwyck in *Double Indemnity* — have been reincarnated in my Bics and Papermates, where they have become integral to my very notion of myself as a writer, that of a risqué, salacious, and even somewhat dissipated voluptuary, not a stiff and formal academic. Although I have never smoked, my ink reeks of tar, of the archaic disapproval we once felt when we saw a Hollywood femme fatale puffing on a Camel and swirling a cocktail in a speakeasy.

My obsessive gesturing with pens is not only part of my homage to Hollywood but is also a manifestation of something that might be called tool homesickness: the irresistible need to have a useful invention in my hands at all times. I engage in a form of literate fidgeting: I doodle constantly and, what's more, with the cap of my pen closed scrawl shapes on my pants and the upholstered furniture around me, an occupational deformity that reveals that, even when I am not writing, I continue to write, treating the world as a blank sheet of paper, an invisible notepad onto which the torrential spate of my words keeps gushing. Human progress is closely related to our ability to make and use tools and so it is not surprising that I feel incomplete unless I am holding one, unless it is attached to me like a Swiss Army knife, which I employ as a multipurpose back scratcher, ear wax remover, cuticle cutter, and, last and perhaps least, writing instrument.

Holding pens or sipping out of tea cups, my pinky erect, also allows me to show off the most conceptual gesture that human beings can make, the movement we use when we thread a needle: the precision gesture, a movement in which we close our thumb and forefinger in a circle to pick up tiny objects, from minute screws in eyeglasses to crumbs on plates. As the subtlest and most thoughtful of movements, it is unique to human beings and hence linked to our physical pride as a species, whose fine motor skills I continue to show off even in situations when they are not required, when I am conversing with others and waving my pen in the air like a baton, scribbling incomprehensible hieroglyphs into empty space. Many of my movements are meant to suggest daintiness and refinement, characteristics that depend largely on the inappropriate display of precision in a context that does not call for it. Oddly enough, this tweezerlike motion, which has, over the centuries, become so important to the hifalutin airs of the would-be aristocrat, probably evolved to enable us to pluck insects out of our fur and pick berries off of thorny bushes, a gesture unlikely to have looked especially refined to other gorillas busily delousing themselves in the dust.

When I am embarrassed, hurt, or angry, I consciously make gestures that will distract viewers from my facial expressions, which I conceal by taking a sip of wine or a bite of food, folding my arms or drumming my fingers on the table, actions that provide a convenient smoke screen for responses that a quivering lip, an angry scowl, or a nervous smile might betray. A new politics of gesturing has led me to invert the whole purpose of certain key bodily movements, which originated as practical reactions to physical stimuli—namely, to the threat of other predators, which made us either head for the hills or stand our ground by squaring our shoulders and gnashing our teeth. The modern response to threat is entirely new and represents nothing short of a revolution in body language: when faced by danger, challenged by a colleague, caught off guard by a comment, or inadvertently insulted by a friend, I do not turn tail and run or stand tall, growling and clawing the air, but instead maintain a false pretense of calm, of lazy nonchalance, refusing to respond to my environment, doing the exact opposite of what gestures were once intended to do, to get us out of harm's way or make our bodies more imposing to our enemies. The new cult of impassivity and easygoing self-confidence, no matter how transparently at odds with our real state of mind, was developed in response to the new conditions under which we experience threat, namely, indoors, between four walls, in contained spaces where we do not have the option to flee or scream at the top of our lungs, and where there are no trees to hide behind. Instead, we have invented a new tree, our faces. We take refuge behind the new power face, the stolid corporate face, which enables us to confront danger through illegibility, sitting patiently in our swivel chairs while our jobs are put on the line and important clients berate us for our incompetence. Living indoors, we do not triumph over our opponents by making large, expansive gestures but by adhering to the strictures of "professionalism," a type of behavior designed for the modern sedentary existence in which the body and its movements are no longer effective in subduing enemies, who do not have sharp fangs and scaly hides but three-piece suits and attaché cases.

When fish detect toxic substances in the water, they automatically close their mouths and shut their gills, a reflex that is directly related to the wincing expression of the human face, which wrinkles its nose and narrows its eyes when it encounters putrid odors that may signal the presence of poisons. Given the evolutionary purpose of the disgust reflex, it would seem that I am constantly assaulted by foul tastes and smells because my face is always shriveling up in a look of nauseated shock, flinching from a world permeated with rotten scents and unpleasant flavors, which I discover in the unlikeliest of places, in the fatuous remarks of strangers, in the deliriousness of goofball comedies, in the turgid pronouncements of postmodern academics, and the pastoral commentaries broadcast on National Public Radio. My world is a compost heap of miasmas from which my sensitive nose is always recoiling, always pretending to catch a gamey whiff of such things as ugly window displays, garish clothing in mail-order catalogues, and bigoted comments by Republican candidates playing to the galleries of right-wing evangelicals.

Many of my gestures and facial expressions have become so detached from their original physiological purpose that they rely on a rhetorical ploy, that our bodies react to the world in a much more direct manner than they really do, that my incredulity at an inappropriate remark is so upsetting to my equilibrium that my elbow slips off the table, that my surprise at an opinion I disagree with is so strong that my chin retracts toward my chest and my face bunches up into a fist, and that the tastelessness of that garish gewgaw in a junk shop fills me with such terror that I raise my eyes beseechingly to the heavens. My gestures are embedded metaphors that evoke a time when our bodies did indeed recoil from powerful physical stimuli, even though the stimulus is now figurative, the threat nonexistent, and there is no urgent need for us to shut our gills and close our mouths in order to avoid swallowing the clouds of mercury and cyanide that used to blanket our spawning grounds during the eruptions of subaqueous volcanos. My gestures hark back to a world in which there really was a clear causal connection between stimulus and response, whereas this link is now simply a colorful conceit, a way of creating an exaggeratedly animated manner in a world so free of threat that our bodies don't usually need to twist and squirm in order to keep out of harm's way.

Perhaps my most conspicuous metaphoric gesture is my laughter, a spasmodic roar in which I become a crash dummy whose head smashes through the windshield in a distinctive whiplash motion, as if the force of someone's wit had hit me like a wave. In order to show my appreciation for the jokes of others, I allow their humor to carom into me like a projectile. Not only do I engage in a mock collision but I knock myself off my own pedestal and undergo a strange kind of class devolution in which my ordinarily elegant demeanor crumbles into a look of vulgar spontaneity. When I laugh, I participate wholeheartedly in a leveling social event in which I give up my superior airs and throw myself into a communal ritual that serves primarily to reinforce the collective spirit of the pack. I hold onto the edges of counters and shake my head as if I were on the verge of collapsing, teeter against walls, bury my chin in the crooks of people's necks, slither down the backs of doors, and pretend that my knees are about to buckle. The democratic ritual of laughter often requires that we symbolically forfeit our physical dignity and degrade ourselves before the group, losing motor control in order to achieve equality on the simplest level of our bodies, whose coordination, whose very ability to remain upright, is seriously compromised.

I am not, however, willing to relinquish my dignity when I smile, especially when I smile for a photographer, who must try every trick in the book to force me to drop my guard and grin, an expression I struggle to suppress, crushing my lips together and eating my smiles so that I often have strange, twisted expressions in photographs, evidence of my largely unsuccessful efforts to remain as static and monumental as the *Mona Lisa*. Unlike other people, I do not want cameras to capture the transitory joys of my life—pedestrian events like opening Christmas presents around the tree or passing Grandma the gravy boat at Thanksgiving—the ephemera of daily living that undercut my belief that every photograph of me is a potential portrait, a document recording my august presence for posterity, an official effigy that will one day occupy its own niche in the pantheon of other immortals. Although my editors and friends don't seem to recognize it, I am a famous person in the making and I jealously preserve my likeness as if I were my reputation's own curator, an image consultant who outlaws smiles, which might disfigure a religious icon that the priests of my future cult will maintain in votive shrines. Only people with an exaggerated sense of their own importance refuse to smile for the camera, an unwillingness that betrays, not shyness, but the arrogance of the crypto-celebrity who shuns the paparazzi and their invasive attempts to photograph him during a relaxed moment, cavorting naked on a beach or dining with friends at a private party, three sheets to the wind.

Although I am bashful and unforthcoming with cameras, I am often obsequious with people and nod obsessively to show that I am listening intently. Nodding is a sign of my intense discomfort with stillness and silence, which I fill by bobbing my head like that of a toy on a spring, troubled by the implications of wordlessness, which calls into question my intelligence and casts doubt on my ability to amuse my friends. Nodding is a false gesture of engagement on my part, however, and often expresses the exact opposite of genuine interest, as can be seen in the fact that my nods are entirely out of synch with what is being said and are scattered randomly throughout my conversations: *"The New York Review of Books* [*nod*] has coverage [*nod, nod*] of this new person who has been elected [*nod*] in the former Soviet Union. They are [*nod, nod*] somewhat ambivalent [*nod*] about him [*nod*]."* What at first sight may appear to be a tic is in fact a way of withdrawing from others, of creating privacy, of putting my chin on automatic pilot so that my mind is free to wander wherever it chooses, to organize the items on my to-do list and indulge in fleeting pornographic fantasies even as my head continues diligently jiggling up and down like the head of a victim of a neurological disorder. By throwing my interlocutor this sop, I prevent him from requiring from me more direct participation in the discussion but at the same time set myself up as the ultimate martyr of garrulousness, the besetting sin of several of my closest friends whose ceaseless prattling I might be able to control if I maintained a more impassive face, which would probably be interpreted as skepticism or disapproval and would therefore elicit attempts to include me in a conversation from which I have allowed myself, out of laziness, to be excluded. My most pressing social problem, that of being reduced to silence, could be solved simply if I chose to remain absolutely still.

It is not the weight of words, however, but gravity itself that forces me to slump so far down in my chair that my head lies against the back of the seat and my butt rests precariously on the outermost edge of the cushion in a position as unlikely as that of a contortionist, a human pretzel who twines himself around his furniture. Whether I am sitting in my recliner or waiting in line in a store, I wage a constant battle against keeping erect. My scholar's stoop is a deformity caused not only by a marked decline in the usefulness of the typical paper-pusher's body, whose arms and legs are less important as manual labor disappears and we give up walking for cars and subways, but also by a major change in the focus of our attention. When we were hunters, we looked straight ahead into the distance, scanning the horizon and the underbrush for prey, but now that we earn our livelihoods in factories and offices,

screwing together motherboards for CPUs and compos-
ing memoranda, our eyes have changed direction, looking *downwards* toward our hands, a shift in point of view
that is entirely reshaping our bodies. If early man
watched other animals, modern man watches his own
hands, the palm-top organizer, the portable play station,
or the microscopic surgical laser for removing brain
tumors and zapping kidney stones. Even our vision has
changed from farsighted to nearsighted, to an efficient
myopia that has evolved so that our sharpest vision is
reserved for things that are within hand's reach, from
the pen moving across the page of my manuscript to the
book lying comfortably in my lap. As one of the most
advanced of a new breed of hand-watchers, my back is
being redesigned to accommodate the inactive life of an
animal that is more of a toolmaker than a hunter, a
future invertebrate who spends all of his time hunched
over, fiddling with his notepads and hunting for a new
type of prey, not food for his stomach, but food for his
angst, his fingernails and cuticles.

All of my life, books have been my teachers, telling me
things I did not know. Given how central school has
been to my life, it is not surprising that when I myself
began to write books, I too assumed the omniscient
voice of the lecturer, not the gabby, laid-back informal-
ity of a friend blabbing about his love affairs on his cell
phone. I do not converse when I write, I declaim, I hold

forth. In fact, when I relax and talk to friends, I relinquish the authority I assume in my books, the vatic tone that some find so chilly, so impersonal, and become painfully vulnerable, tongue-tied, incoherent, stuttering through sentences many people are too impatient to allow me to finish. The angels that are said to cause the unnerving silences that cast shadows over our conversations not only pass overhead in my case, they circle like vultures.

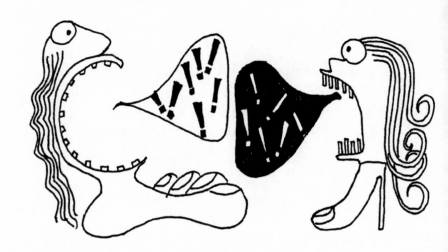

7

Speaking/Listening

When I was twelve, my family moved from Wisconsin to the very heart of Appalachia, where men with sawed-off shotguns and coon caps, as my adolescent imagination chose to misrepresent them, spoke such a thick Southern brogue that my sisters and I were hard-pressed to understand the simplest greetings or the most matter-of-fact requests. I looked down on this incomprehensible drawl and resolved never to acquire it, a decision I put into effect by making a tape of all the vowel sounds and a handful of key phrases of the rain-in-Spain-falls-mainly-on-the-plain variety, which I repeated in order to keep my voice free of the unmusical intonations of the hillbilly. When other teenagers were listening to the Monkees and Mama Cass, I was listening to recordings of my own voice during a series of self-imposed language labs, remedial drills in which, perhaps for the last time in my entire life, I was able to hear myself without cringing, without shuddering at my stilted phraseology and prematurely aged stateliness.

The result of this self-administered speech therapy has been an entirely manufactured style of delivery, a fake patrician voice that many people, much to my embarrassment, have mistaken for a British accent but that in fact derives from Hollywood, from the back lots of MGM, from years and years of watching reruns. As a self-conscious fop who associated the Appalachian twang with ignorance and, what's more, with the hatred of homosexuals, I created an ultrasophisticated set of imaginary peers, free of prejudices, by speaking in the hifalutin manner of Grace Kelly and Norma Shearer, whose studied graciousness and aristocratic bearing helped me eradicate all traces of the region in which I lived. In imitation of the faux Brits in classic American cinema, where members of the upper classes often seem to have come straight from the cricket fields of Eton, no matter how many years they lived in Bensonhurst and the Bronx, I began to overarticulate shamelessly, dotting every *i*, crossing every *t*, and pronouncing every consonant so that, to this day, the words I use seem to have several more syllables than in fact they do.

Although it is as difficult to change one's voice as it is to change one's handwriting, I have tried conscientiously to suppress the sound of my pretentiousness, but in the process I have created further distortions in my speech. I pour on the plain American accent so unconvincingly that at times my voice cracks like a pubescent boy's, the mellifluousness of the elegant gay man giving way to the abrupt, hard-boiled delivery of a character out of a Raymond Chandler novel. I deflate myself at every turn by speaking in an artificially brusque manner and by littering my speech with profanities, which lose their vituperative power when they are tossed off with self-conscious precision. I am a peculiarly ineffective swearer because I curse according to an agenda, that of the self-saboteur who, in an effort to sound less affected, to get down with the boyz in the hood, punctures his airs by showering his audience with scatological and sacrilegious epithets. I never drop the *g* in "fucking," allow the "of" to become "uv" in "sonuvabitch," elide the *r*'s in "motherfucker" to form the colorfully thuggish "mothafucka," or say "faggit" like a genuine gay basher, but instead curse like an elocutionist who lambastes his enemies as if he were reciting a poem. My primary reason for swearing is not to express anger but to sully my own image, to throw mud pies in the mirror, as if I had never been to Harvard or written four books or lectured on college campuses, as if I were a drunken sailor rather than just a gutter-mouthed intellectual trying hopelessly to talk tough, to prove to others that, his insufferable pomposity notwithstanding, he has cracked as many dirty jokes in as many locker rooms as the next guy.

But although I pepper my conversation with obscenities, my middle-class upbringing emerges in one of my characteristic expressions, "Whoopsy," an annoyingly flaccid expletive that I use when, in the presence of others, I make a mistake or damage someone else's property. "Whoopsy" is not a curse but an apology, a word that I utter out of guilt, not rage, attempting to endear myself to the owner of the fountain pen I've just broken or the wine goblet I've just smashed, adopting the inappropriately youthful jargon of a bobby-soxer from the 1950s. When we make a mistake in front of a witness who might, with good reason, find fault with our ham-handedness, we automatically infantilize ourselves in an effort to make light of the situation, uttering the wide-eyed exclamation of a choirboy or a cheerleader. By slipping into a style that is both puerile and anachronistic when I drop something or snap it in two, I forestall the criticisms of the peevish lawyer whose brief I accidentally erased or the friend whose white sofa I stained with Burgundy wine, for how can any civilized person in good conscience attack a trembling teenager who shuffles his feet, lowers his eyes, and mutters such things as "Golly," "Gee whiz," and "Whoopsy"?

But if I damage something and there *are* no witnesses, especially if I damage something of my own, I drop the teenybopper routine and let fly with "Damnitalltohell-goddamnit." When we are alone, we have no reason to wriggle out of guilt or appease our critics and hence we do not address them at all but rather direct our aggression towards the inanimate thing itself, much as people kick the doors on which they have stubbed their toes or slam down phones that have just delivered bad news, thereby killing the messenger. Rather than accepting responsibility for the disaster, apologizing for my clumsiness, or turning myself into a childish innocent, I scold the jammed stapler or the shattered vase. I even administer corporal punishment to them and engage in a nonsensical form of anthropomorphism in which I cast myself as the victim, not the perpetrator, the blameless dupe of that willful tea cup or that disobedient CD player, which I reprimand for *its* awkwardness, *its* incompetence. Accidents thus elicit two linguistic responses from me, one for when I feel I must pacify angry bystanders by adopting a simpering, adolescent manner and one for when there is no one in the room to hear me viciously berate objects I scream at like a frenzied child beater brandishing a wire coat hanger.

I am not always so free with my language. As I have become more prolix on paper, I have become more stammering as a speaker. I apply to conversation literary standards derived from prose, rules of correctness and elegance that are inapplicable to the hasty improvisations of everyday speech, which one cannot redraft, edit on a word processor, and reprint, blackening the page of one's manuscripts with deletions and insertions. I am, for instance, a studied connoisseur of the *mot juste*, which I never light on effortlessly, as if by chance, but ferret out only by combing through my internal thesaurus, where I fall into a morass of alternatives that leads me to stutter, to repeat definite and indefinite articles as many as four or five times as I hesitate over the various choices that come to mind: "the . . . the . . . the . . . the . . . silken tresses on the . . . the . . . the . . . vixen's head," "that . . . that . . . grotesque eyesore affixed to that . . . that . . . that . . . monstrosity of a building," or "a . . . a . . . a . . . mantra, a chant, of encouragement." Unlike those who suffer from real *psychological* speech impediments, a handicap that makes them trip over the initial consonants of words, sputtering out alliterative volleys of plosives, dentals, and diphthongs, I suffer from a *literary* speech impediment which forces me to repeat the articles of nouns that are never on the tip of my tongue, delightfully serendipitous, but that I must summon out of the abyss like a frustrated conjurer. My ceaseless endeavors to track down the perfect word have actually increased my incoherence rather than making me the silver-tongued orator I aspire to be.

It is a truism of contemporary creative writing classes that good prose reflects our real voices, but in my case, the opposite is true: talking is only an inferior, poorly written form of my writing. Prose is not speech in slow motion — speech is writing speeded up, played at an accelerated pace that shows all of the old drafts, the mass of editorial scribbles that authors hide from their readers, maintaining the pretense that their prose flows from their pens and pencils without a single blot or erasure. Writers have a unique perspective on language that makes them highly critical when they are forced to listen to their own conversation, which never measures up to the idealized world of the page. In this utopian realm, one always finds the right adjective, risks metaphors without falling flat on one's face, and speaks in complete sentences that have beginnings, middles, and ends and don't straggle off into blathering, inconclusive nonsense. Moreover, one's false starts, one's errors of judgment and taste, are read only by that most discreet and supportive of critics, the waste basket.

I falter over my words not only because I bring a distinctly belletristic sensibility to the mundane chitchat of my interactions with store clerks and bus drivers but because I simply cannot master the extensive vocabulary of modern life, from the motherboards, microchips, and servomechanisms in our PCs to the platelets, lymphocytes, and isoantibodies in our blood. I am therefore constantly resorting to a generic noun, a word that functions as an invitation to my listeners to fill in the blank: the empty cipher "thing," as in "I left the . . . the thing on the coffee table," i.e., the remote control; "bring me the . . . thing," i.e., the chicken mallet; or "could you move that thing closer to the other thing?," i.e., the toaster to the electrical outlet. Unable to remember the simplest words, I frequently play a version of twenty questions in which I enlist my friends in the task of helping me to guess what I'm thinking of, an anxious game of mind reading in which I become a helplessly animated charadist who is forced to sculpt spheres and boxes in the air, forms that usually baffle my listeners, who stare dumbfounded as I attempt to hunt down such esoteric words as "refrigerator," "battery," and "light-bulb." The material complexity of our lives and our growing number of possessions pose an enormous epistemological challenge that is increasingly leaving us at a loss for words, forcing us to revert to a prelinguistic form of communication. Both the absence of nouns in the lives of the earliest *Homo sapiens* and their super-abundance in the lives of contemporary city dwellers have the same consequence, a strange new stutter that we are now overcoming by using sign language, reverting to a primitive system of speechless gestures, pointing and gesticulating in order to conjure up the word "microwave," "laptop," or "halogen lamp."

Not only are there too many things in my world, there are too many people: movie stars, politicians, third-rate hosts of game shows, defrocked Southern ministers, drug-addicted supermodels — a madding crowd of celebrities whom I can never identify, handicapped as I am by a pathological name block, a shortcoming that, at its worst, has prevented me from remembering the names of my own mother and boyfriend. The problem is so severe that I am frequently trapped in a double or even triple bind, a vicious linguistic circle in which I jog my failing memory by calling up the name of someone related to "that guy with the big nose who's dating what's-her-name, the star of that show everyone's watching, what's it called?"; or "that televangelist formerly married to the other one, that dragon lady who wears all of that mascara that trickles down her cheeks when she cries on cue." A source of continual humiliation and a huge waste of time and mental energy, my block derives in part from my lack of public contact, from my dislike of collective living, an insularity that has never required me to develop a knack for names, which slip through my fingers like water. My world is eerily free of proper nouns, populated solely by faces, dim shades who flit in and out of my life with every new box office hit and runaway *New York Times* best-seller. My name block also reflects the explosive development of popular culture, which has placed huge strains on the human memory by exposing us to more people than we have ever known in the history of the species — the drunk, yo-yo-dieting adulterers of scandal sheets, late-night talk shows, and teenage fanzines, an entire class of insignificant stars that occupies far too much of our long-term memories.

If my overtaxed neuro-circuits have contributed to my faltering style, so has my conscious decision to reduce such filler as "like," "um," "man," "dude," "kewl," and "you know what I'm saying" — conversational filler that now constitutes the better part of the speech of a generation eager to express tribal unity through hip colloquialisms. But though I have weeded out much of this filler from my speech, by no means have I eliminated it altogether, mainly because it reflects deep-seated anxieties that I share with the rest of my society, as in the case of the expression "I mean": "I was exhausted by the end; I mean, I was bored out of my fucking gourd, it was so dull. He maundered on for over an hour. I mean, really! What was he thinking?" Like most people, I am always acting as a self-commentator, an emcee who narrates his own speech even as he talks, checking to see if he has made himself clear, if he has "connected," if such conceptually crude statements as "it took forever; I mean, the traffic was awful" or "the weather is unbearable; I mean, I am dying from the heat" have been fully understood. This obsessive act of self-elucidation, performed even when we state the obvious, is grounded in our profound doubts that communication has indeed occurred, that we have reached listeners who seem separated from us by endless misapprehensions. The result is an almost neurotic tendency to paraphrase, to footnote our platitudes, as if our conversation were so difficult that we must function as a simultaneous translator.

The question "you know?" also elicits from our audience verbal confirmation that we are thinking along the same lines and that nothing we have said is out of bounds or contrary to reason. When I talk, I frequently defer in passing to a body of common knowledge. Dispersing "you know" 's at every turn, I posit the existence of shared experiences so universal that their truth can be taken for granted, since everything we utter is, as we ourselves make clear, already "known," instantaneously recognized by our peers. The repetition of this expression fosters the illusion of identity between the speaker and the listener who belong to a homogeneous culture, whereas in fact we live in an increasingly diverse and fractured society in which we can never be certain whether our audience does indeed "know" the truth of what we have spoken. "You know" ultimately becomes a command, not an inquiry, an official decree that tries to legislate conformity linguistically by broadcasting the subliminal message "You are like me, you know what I know," thus inventing with words a unanimity that simply does not exist. An instrument of homogenization rather than a confirmation of real social harmony, the litany of "you know" 's scattered throughout our speech expresses a peculiarly modern form of paranoia, a fear that we are talking, not with replicas of ourselves who speak with a single voice, but with perfect strangers.

My strategies for strengthening consensus are complemented by a wide array of phrases meant to convey frankness, an admirable trait that, as an unapologetic liar who avoids public confrontations at all cost, I cannot by any stretch of the imagination claim as one of my primary virtues. My conversation is, however, clogged with the rhetoric of candor, with such doughty expressions of openness as "to tell you the truth," "I'll have to say," "the truth is," "I'm going to level with you," "quite honestly," and "to be perfectly frank." I also exaggerate my capacity to get to the heart of the matter by sprinkling my speech with such adverbs as "essentially," "simply," "in fact," "literally," and "actually," words that suggest that I have an almost Socratic ability to show others that things are not as they seem and that I alone am uniquely qualified to rip the wool off people's eyes. As someone who has little place for honesty in his life and who conceals his caustic nature at every turn in order to avoid being ostracized as a cynic, I am nonetheless always playing the role of the guileless debunker of falsehoods who shoots straight from the hip, letting the world know precisely what's on his mind. One of our cherished illusions as speakers is that, unlike others, we don't mince words, that we are our culture's conscience, its gadflies, idealists who assume the moral high ground in the war against hypocrisy and cant. This self-righteous drama of uncompromising gutsiness is among the highest forms of self-flattery in a society dependent on politesse, especially in the case of someone like me who has learned to camouflage his often acerbic opinions and nod in amiable if noncommittal agreement every time a friend sings the praises of astrology, Ross Perot, the pope, and twelve-step programs.

We may enjoy convincing people that we are intolerant of deliberately misleading statements but at heart we are all Orwellian double-talkers who delight in imprecision. I undercut my own arrogance by using filler that strikes a note of uncertainty—"sort of," "kind of," "I guess," "maybe," "apparently," and "it seems to me"— expressions that are meant to humble us, to bring us down to the level of others, to impugn our authority as speakers so that we can submerge ourselves in the linguistic status quo, in a democracy of ineloquence: "It was sort of, you know, I guess maybe kind of silly for me to do what I did" and "We, um, kind of ignored him because he was, I guess you could say, sort of rude to us, it seemed to me." We distrust glibness so completely that we actively model ourselves on the negative ideal of the mumbling imbecile who utters one obscurity after the next and therefore never distinguishes himself from the herd, which loathes smart talk as evidence of snobbish self-assurance, the presumptuousness of the elitist who breaks rank and defies the low standards of egalitarian incoherence jealously maintained by his peers. Filler helps us to dumb ourselves down so we don't seem too vain or individualistic but aspire instead to keep ourselves in line with the lowest common denominator, with anti-intellectual philistines who actively strive to preserve their inexpressiveness.

Just as the Alaskan Inuits are said to have at least twenty ways of saying "snow," the very element of their lives, so I have at least twenty ways of saying "goodbye," the very element of mine, as is apparent during protracted phone conversations, which I am always hastening to a curt conclusion, begging to get off the line and return to my reading and writing. My misanthropy becomes painfully obvious in the expressions I use to wriggle out of gab sessions that have no clear exit and that I therefore terminate by stating, "I have to run," "We'll talk later," "I'm expecting a call," "Well, listen, I've got to go," "We'll have to talk soon," and "I'll be in touch." Whereas my greetings consist mostly of "Hello,"

"Hey," "Hi," "How are you?," and "What's up?," I draw upon a broad range of synonyms for "Farewell," a fact that suggests how uncomfortable I am during conversations and how I yearn for something I now recognize as one of my most precious possessions: the luxury of silence.

Listening

My two stock responses to the comments of others are hilarity and disbelief. The highest form of flattery in a society that has elevated the figure of the comedian to a position once occupied by the high priest is braying laughter, the guffaws with which I explode when I am in the presence of someone who frightens me and whom I appease by playing my own built-in sound track, disguising my insecurity behind the titters of shrill merriment. Similarly, I flatter my friends by feigning surprise and treating every comment about the aggravations of the weather and the skyrocketing price of gasoline as a startling revelation, a disclosure I acknowledge by saying "Wow," "Really?!!," "No!," "Imagine!," "Strange," "Gosh!," and even (although very seldom) "That's so weird!" Surprise is a way of dramatizing the significance of our friends' statements, which we pretend are so amazing that we stand dumbstruck, our mouths gaping, stopped dead in our tracks by such uncanny pronouncements as "My allergies are acting up" and "I had to take my cat to the vet." The surprise topos ultimately has an anesthetizing effect on our conversation and, to some extent, on our thinking as well. It forces us to adopt a position of false naïveté in which we inadvertently cretinize ourselves and lower our tolerance for the genuinely surprising, so accustomed are we to responding, with the same magnitude of astonishment, to news of a sprained ankle and an eyewitness account of an ax murder. Not only has this convention weakened our capacity to experience wonder and numbed us to a world that provides myriad occasions in which we genuinely should be astonished, but it has created a new set of clichés that actually mean the opposite of what they are supposed to mean, namely, "That's not surprising at all, that's banal; I have absolutely no reaction whatsoever to what you just said." When we express surprise, it is almost certain that what we are really feeling is stupefaction and obliviousness.

Surprise has become a reflex for someone who carefully suppresses responses he has learned others will find unkind and embittered. If my speech bears the disfiguring hallmarks of my writing, my writing bears the scars of my insecurity as a speaker. I am such a polemical and abrasive writer in part because I fail entirely to be candid with my friends, who force me into the role of an amen chorus, a fawning claque that laughs when it is expected to laugh, commiserates when it is expected to commiserate, and expresses sympathetic outrage when it is expected to be outraged. The result is an overpowering internal monologue, a *sub*conversation where my real reactions are occurring and where the outwardly

obedient yes-man talks back, rebelling against his passivity. My prose taps into this reservoir of unspoken
responses and gives voice to the resentment I stifle in
my daily interactions with others, which I view as so
tragically flawed that I have invented a realm in which
I live out thwarted fantasies of being forthright, even
blunt. My prose thus stands in a pathological relation to
my speech, which has become the troubled muse of my
satirical style, the protective armor that allows the introverted yes-man to become the naysayer, to step out of
the tightly serried ranks of the amen chorus and take his
rightful place as a participant and not just a victim of the
spate of words in which I often feel I am drowning.

While my more confident friends have exiled me to the
audience, well beyond the glare of the footlights in which
they so self-indulgently hold forth, I by no means remain
silent in my seat but engage in what might be called noisy
listening, a type of rapt attention in which I make a kind
of affirmative murmur, a steady stream of such insincere if
unfailingly effective prompts as "Uh-huh, really, oh,
mmmmmm, yes, uh-huh, okay, all right, great." Although
I am reduced to silence, I continue offering assurances
that I am tuned in and that my interlocutor has my permission to proceed, even when I long, above all else, to
revoke this permission and restore balance to a conversation that, with my implied consent, has become unjustly
unilateral. As an audience in revolt, I try to curb this
incessant drone by refusing to vary it, as I do when I am
more genuinely engaged, expressing my absorption by

alternating my "Oh" 's with "Ah" 's and "Um" 's, my "Okay" 's with "I see" 's and "Well" 's, my "All right" 's with "Uh-huh" 's and "Yes" 's. When I cease listening and my blood pressure begins to rise as garrulous friends ramble on, criminally heedless of the impatience written all over my face, I lapse into a state of passive aggression and cease varying my soothing burble of assent, which I allow to become as mechanical and monotonous as possible. Like a metronome, I repeat "Uh-huh, uh-huh" at carefully measured intervals, all in the futile expectation that the person yakking at me will notice that he is talking to a tape recording.

Noisy listening has always been a part of common courtesy, but nineteenth- and twentieth-century technology has inflated its importance. Before the invention of the telephone, we were probably much more silent when we listened because we could rely on visual cues like nods, eye contact, and facial expressions. The telephone has created a visual vacuum that we fill with noise—with cluckings of the tongue, tsk-tsks, and grunts of agreement. The telephone has not changed the way we talk so much as the way we listen, exaggerating the auditory dimension of conversation and instilling us with new fears of silence, the uncomfortable pauses that reverberate far more clamorously in the limbo of fiber optics than in the far less ambiguous realm of face-to-face encounters.

As dissatisfied as I am with my role as a doormat that conveniently stretches itself across the threshold of every talkative person I know, I cannot bring myself to violate what I have come to recognize as a major taboo in our society: the taboo against a listener's complete silence, a law we break only under very unusual circumstances, specifically, in a theater, a church, or a lecture hall, buildings equipped with proscenium arches, pulpits, and podiums — architectural monuments to the temporary suspension of this basic rule of dialogue. Garrulous people can tyrannize us only if we let them, if we offer our noisy listening, for once we clam up and refuse to provide our meager encouragement of "Oh" 's and "Uh-huh" 's, all pretense of conversation is abandoned and the speaker automatically transgresses the injunction against soliloquizing. Not even the most courageous (or the most oblivious) chatterbox can continue talking if the listener plays dead, breaks eye contact, refuses to nod, or withholds his compulsive murmur, an act of civil disobedience that immediately transforms dialogue into an oration and hence traps the speaker in an untenable position, that of talking to himself, jabbering out loud to an empty room. The problem with playing dead is that it is a supremely difficult role to perform because the taboo works both ways, at once forbidding the speaker from proceeding without the listener's compliance and enjoining the listener to continue inciting the speaker, whom we cannot simply abandon there alone out on the stage, slipping back into our seats in the darkened auditorium rather than assuming the subordinate position of the hero's sidekick, like the maids and butlers in classical dramas. Anyone who has ever held the telephone receiver at arm's length while an exasperating busybody launches into a blustering diatribe knows how difficult it is to keep from offering polite responses, so concerned are we about hurting the feelings of the speaker, who almost invariably will utter a panic-stricken "Hello?!" after thirty seconds of dead air. Perhaps the solution to my most pressing social dilemma is not more speech but more silence, an intrepid refusal to participate in a virtually unbreakable pact, an orgy of mindless agreement, a brutal if bloodless war of words.

8

Farting, Pooping, Peeing, and Bathing

Like the majority of people, I enjoy the odor of my own farts. I have been a confirmed fart smeller ever since childhood, when I was introduced to the art by my mother, who engaged in farting contests with coarse male friends, setting an uninhibitedly vulgar example for her three children, who on long car trips cultivated their skills as connoisseurs by naming their emissions such things as "buttermilk," "chocolate," "cabbage," and "pineapple upside-down cake." Naturally, my enjoyment of this pastime has never extended to smelling other people's nor, above all else, to other people smelling mine, as happens so often at work when, mistakenly assuming the coast is clear, I silently exude a toxic cloud of sulfurous gas, only to watch horrified as unsuspecting colleagues wade straight through this invisible miasma, an expression of polite if unconvincing obliviousness etched on their faces.

Why do I feel so guilty and embarrassed when I fart in public and yet so secretly thrilled when I fart alone at home, flapping the covers while I lie in bed in order to get the full aroma, reveling in the intimate stench of my body? The scents of our nether regions have probably never been as delectably forbidden as they are now, after over a century of hygienic crusades that have transformed public farting into an antisocial crime, a grotesque indiscretion that was once practiced with relative impunity before modern scientists established the empirical link between human waste and disease. Once this association was firmly planted in our minds by early bacteriologists, who finally discovered the origin of such water-borne epidemics as cholera and typhoid, stark divisions opened up between our public and private selves, and previously admissible, if uncouth, behaviors were driven into a dark, domestic underground, where they flourish like the rites of a secret scatological sect. In fact, it is safe to say that, perfumed with the irresistible fragrance of guilt, farts smell far better today than ever before in the history of mankind.

The fact that I must now mask my scents so completely in public with deodorants, colognes, and mouthwashes has stimulated the intense delight I feel in unmasking them in private, in exploring hidden aromas that remain tucked away in tiny crevices of unwashed flesh. When I am at home, my hands restlessly roam over my entire body in search of any lingering odors that I may have overlooked, raking through my pubic hairs in order to pick up traces of sweat and digging fragrant lint out of my belly button, only to lift the tips of my fingers to my nose. In an age in which people bathed as little as once a year, in which many believed that contact with soil was actually healthy, and in which toilet paper consisted of balls of rolled hay called mempiria, or even of a curved stick designed for scraping one's hole clean, hung in the outhouse for general use (hence, the deceptively banal expression "the wrong end of the stick"), it is unlikely that people enjoyed their bodily odors with the obscene relish that I do. Appearances to the contrary, I do not actually smell myself with my nose but with my fingertips, which must be sent out like reconnoitering parties to survey the lay of the land, delving into my armpits, scrounging for slimy excretions behind my testicles, scratching scaly patches of dandruff, harvesting toe jam, and gouging out minute quantities of ear wax, which inevitably get smeared in streaks across the pages of my manuscripts. Before the twentieth century, people bathed so infrequently that it was perfectly possible for them (and, for that matter, anyone unfortunate enough to stand within a ten-foot radius) to smell their bodies with their own noses, but now that we shower every day, we are forced to smell ourselves with our fingers, which have become extensions of the olfactory nerve, traveling noses with Maybelline nails that explore every nook and cranny of our bodies in hopes of finding some telltale remnant of intoxicating filth.

One key part of my rebellion against modern hygiene lies fermenting in those sheets I flap like a wind machine when I fart. I wash them at most once every two months, in part because I will drag myself to the laundromat only when I have reached the very bottom of what is perhaps the largest underwear collection in the Northeast, and in part because I actually enjoy wallowing in this sweaty sty, burrowing into a rat's nest of tangled blankets and stained comforters that have absorbed my distinctive odor. Perhaps because I have polluted my bed, leaked semen into the mattress, and left greasy stains on my pillow cases, I have made it unfit for any other creature to inhabit. I have marked my territory through defilement, a form of hygienic terrorism crucial to the way in which we strengthen our sense of ownership. Performing acts of environmental pollution is one of my chief techniques for creating privacy, which has been subtly diminished by modern standards of cleanliness. New ideals of sterility require us to eliminate our presence from our surroundings and thus thwart our desire to dominate and control our lairs by making our rooms as olfactorily unique — and hence as unacceptable to others — as possible. One of the reasons housework and bathing are such chores for me is that they are psychologically complex tasks fraught with tension between my hygienic superego, the resident civil servant who goes around disinfecting his armpits and sheets out of respect for public health, and the resident caged beast who goes around lifting his leg at every fire hydrant in his apartment in order to leave his malodorous name tag on the entire inventory of his possessions.

Aside from farting and obsessive self-fondling, the other major activities I will perform only behind locked doors are, of course, shitting and peeing, which bring out in me the fastidious feline hiding its feces in its litter box, building a tiny tumulus for its turds. Throughout my childhood, I required so much privacy for my daily constitutional that I was unable even to enter public bathrooms and was forced to hold it in for twelve-hour stretches on cross-country trips, so appalled was I by the conditions of shit-splattered gas station johns, which I avoided at all costs, much to the detriment of my bladder, which still suffers the consequences of having been stretched like a beach ball by my timidity. To this day, I am a hopeless victim of that most emasculating of phobias, pee shyness, and detest urinals, which I consider a monument to careless masculine hygiene, to the immodesty of the exhibitionistic Neanderthal, who feels no compunction whatsoever about unzipping, whipping it out, and letting it fly.

The taboo against shitting and peeing in public is a relatively recent one. As late as the nineteenth century, people still followed the basic rule of thumb that one should retire to a distance of a "bow's shot" from any human habitation in order to relieve oneself, and even affluent ladies visiting their country houses were permitted to crap in their well-manicured gardens, a practice quaintly known as "plucking a rose." After thousands of years of pooping in the presence of other members of our tribe, we suddenly feel a pressing desire to hide our functions, to enter a special contemplative cell where we sit on the throne lost in a trance, our heads lowered prayerfully over our haunches, furious when the urgent call of nature leads another family member to interrupt our hushed meditations with angry pleas to hurry up. In other words, the luxurious solitude I feel locked in my bathroom is not the result of an animal need to hide from others while pooping (indeed, few animals hide when they shit) but is an historically datable sentiment related to a governmental campaign to drive people indoors away from public outhouses perched on bridges that emptied directly into a city's water supply and from open cesspools that, after torrential downpours, overflowed into the streets. Sitting in my quiet cubicle, I am not alone at all, for the state is in the bathroom with me, guiding every step of a ritual that, while it may seem secretive and personal, is actually the result of an internalized public health initiative launched by nineteenth-century hygienists. The taboo against public defecation has created highly utilitarian shame about being seen by others and has thus created the psychological conditions of bashfulness conducive to containing human waste.

The hypnotic coziness I feel in my bathroom is intensified by the fact that I read while shitting, most often books of history but, when visiting others, collections of cartoons, the dominant genre of the typical lavatory library, which consists largely of jokes suitable for the short duration of time we spend in the john as well as the nature of the activities we perform there. Such titles as *101 Uses for a Dead Cat* and *The Barf 'n' Booger Book* are so popular next to the commode because shitting and peeing are democratic, leveling experiences and the toilet seat the throne of Everyman, an appropriately unregal place in which to contemplate our common humanity by perusing deflating cartoons about bodily functions. The comic nature of bathroom literature also expresses a characteristically modern discomfort with our excretions, constituting the nervous giggle with which an antiseptic age approaches the insurmountable challenges of its unrealistically fastidious hygiene, especially now that the outhouse has been grafted right onto our living quarters, becoming a well-appointed extension of our bedrooms and kitchens. Because of this new proximity, we have buried the old outhouse beneath the euphemisms of the new "comfort station" with its distinctly feminine, pink decor, shag-rug toilet seat covers, Daisy-Mate bath decals, and even humorous bathroom reading, which hides the ugliness of shit behind the adolescent titters of the disquieted prankster who is still adjusting to our culture's elevated standards of cleanliness.

Like those who examine their boogers on their fingers before popping them into their mouths (another of my — and I suspect, my reader's — nasty habits), I stare into the toilet bowl after I poop, fascinated with these enigmatic productions, which disappear so mysteriously, whisked away into the depths of subterranean plumbing. Just as our interest in our bodily odors has increased as we have become cleaner, so our love affair with our excretions has developed into a full-blown crush now that we see less of them around us, bobbing in cesspools, coiled in porcelain chamber pots, and lying in the gutters where they were once tossed out with the morning "slops" on the heads of unwary passersby, who occasionally took the precaution of walking with umbrellas or heavy overcoats in order to avoid the cataracts of urine and excrement that splashed out of second-story windows. Sanitation has deprived us of a key form of knowledge about our bodies and therefore heightened our curiosity about a substance that people once touched on a daily basis. Familiarity bred contempt, whereas we now look almost longingly into that gurgling vortex as our stools are hurtled down pipes that disgorge into hidden grottoes seen only in old movies.[1]

---

[1] It is worth noting that Freud spent most of his adult life in a world without internal plumbing, which was available only to the well-to-do in the late nineteenth century and to the middle classes in the 1920s and 1930s. While his wealthy Viennese clients may have had running water and spacious WCs stocked with luxurious toiletries, he himself was the son of a lower-middle-class merchant who slept with his eight children in a single room in a cramped apartment. His theories about potty training and his elaborate allegory of excrement and anal retentiveness emerged before the development of the modern bathroom, in an era in which shit couldn't be disposed of with a simple yank of a chain and was probably as omnipresent in the streets—as well as on the soles of people's shoes—as dog poop. Freud's ideas may be the product of a particular moment in architectural history and may therefore be psychologically irrelevant to an age that has witnessed the triumph of chrome fixtures, Moist Wipes, Tidy Bowl, and running water. For the last century, we have been fixated on theories whose intellectual underpinnings may be primitive plumbing and bad hygiene, conditions that gave rise to fears and obsessions that have been significantly relieved, not by decades of soul searching on a sofa, but by a much less expensive form of psychoanalysis, the "siphon jet flushing action" of the indoor toilet.

Instead of fearing shit, I suffer from another, entirely irrational fear, that one day I will become a street person, a fantasy stimulated not only by anxieties about my ability to support myself as a writer but also by their direct corollary, the shocking hygiene of bums so ripe that they empty subway cars and force pedestrians to take a wide berth around them as they squat on the sidewalks muttering to themselves in urine-soaked rags. The image of the derelict, drunk and incontinent, plays a significant role in my hygienic fantasy life, partly because I rarely saw such pariahs in the relatively small cities in which I grew up, and partly because street people are to the middle class what the poorhouse was to the Victorians: a frightening vision of Christmases to Come, of life after bankruptcy, when, the bottom having fallen out of our finances, we are driven into the streets, where we are stripped of our last badge of respectability, our cleanness. These itinerant figures haunt my nightmares as emblems of economic failure, which is more intimately linked than ever to bad hygiene. An enormous gap has developed between the grooming of the public at large and that of the average bag lady scratching furiously at her matted hair. It is not as if street people are significantly dirtier than they were in past centuries but simply that most of us are far cleaner and hence more disgusted by the unnerving sight of a fellow creature wallowing in his own excretions, a spectacle that would have been far less disturbing when the hygiene of the bum and that of the bourgeois were not so spectacularly different. The beggar also inspires more revulsion than ever before in human history because public sources of water have all but disappeared—pumps, wells, public baths, subway johns, facilities that became extinct with the privatization of plumbing and the growth of the household bathroom, which have deprived street people of their very means of getting clean, forcing them to sneak into the toilets of McDonald's and Wendy's for disastrous immersions.

Another monster lurks in my bathroom: the Hollywood slasher. As a member of a generation that came of age after *Psycho*, I cannot bathe with the same peace of mind as those who never heard the screeching score that played as Anthony Perkins carved up Janet Leigh one dark night at the Bates Motel. Why do I experience a fleeting fear of intruders the moment I turn on the taps of my shower? Hitchcock may have invented the classic "shower scene" but he was merely responding to popular apprehensions and to the dramatic potential of the physical setting itself: the clinical lighting, the white tile (perfect for showing blood), the sound of running water blocking out stealthy footsteps and creaking doors, and the fact that the bather is naked, whereas the murderer is fully dressed (often overdressed, wearing sunglasses, a floppy bonnet, and a Burberry raincoat). I am also susceptible to slasher fantasies in the bathroom because, in the course of the last century, everyone from our homeroom teacher to our pastor has instilled in us a new degree of shame about our hygiene, making us feel as if we can never get clean enough, as if we are doing something furtive in front of those steamy mirrors in which we first make out the ski mask and the gleaming blade. Slasher fears are rooted in the evolution of this architectural space from a drafty outhouse into a quiet inner sanctum that affords complete privacy and forbids prying eyes, a tranquil retreat in which we luxuriate in a type of embarrassed, beleaguered solitude that breeds fears of the sudden disruption of privacy, of an intruder barging in without knocking. One of the basic scenes of contemporary cinema neatly encapsulates the entire history of modern hygiene and the radical transformation of an outdoor stall with a rickety door often dangling from its hinges into a contemplative cell, the site of unmentionable practices that others once witnessed in public baths or even around the kitchen sink but that are now so solitary that they create violent images of interruption.

The psychological nature of our experiences in the bathroom can also be seen in the fact that, no matter how clean I am in actuality, I feel absolutely filthy if I do not shower before a certain well-established time in the day, even though my life is by nature antiseptic, since it is impossible to work up much of a sweat turning the pages of books or reclining in my armchair. Within a matter of an hour or two after my regularly scheduled late-afternoon shower, an internal alarm is tripped and my skin suddenly feels sticky and grimy, my face greasy, and my scalp itchy and dry, despite the fact that the chances are very slim that I am any grubbier at seven o'clock than I was at four or five. My hygiene is on a timer that has nothing to do with the state of my body but with my emotions and conscience, with the conviction that I have been derelict in my duties even if I have allowed only a few hours to pass after I customarily perform my daily ablutions. *Feeling* dirty has nothing to do with *being* dirty. We shower because of guilt, not grime, the difference between washing once a day and washing every other day or even twice a week being in most respects undetectable to anyone other than ourselves.

Given that the cult of cleanliness is little more than a century old, it is surprising how the original motivation for hygiene, controlling disease and protecting ourselves from contamination, has disappeared so completely from our consciousness that we no longer even know why we bathe and believe instead that the bathtub is a spa or an isolation chamber in which we relax and refresh ourselves rather than get clean. Within the course of only five or six generations, the scientific basis for the taboo against dirt has been forgotten, mainly because the black plague, smallpox, and cholera have all but disappeared in the First World and the death rates from infectious diseases have plummeted. Worries of illness have been supplanted in our minds by a much more intangible fear than the specter of germs, the fear of social ostracism, of stinking in public without knowing it, of being excluded from respectable society as a nose-picking, fart-smelling persona non grata with halitosis and dandruff, a fate that a consumerist society exploits by barraging us with images of forsaken flops parked beside telephones that never ring. As someone

who spends most of his time alone, I receive relatively little information from others about the state of my hygiene,
a fact that explains my obsession with brushing my teeth
(as many as seven or eight times a day) and gargling with
no less than four separate brands of candy-flavored
mouthwashes and antiplaque "oral rinses," an arsenal that
suggests that I have a distinctly self-involved attitude
towards my mouth. My exaggerated fear of dragon breath
stems from the absence of public checks in my life, of the
means of verifying the condition of my body, a self-incog-
nizance that leads to frantic gestures of overcompensa-
tion, which have taken their toll on my irritated gums,
receding from decades of overbrushing. No sooner do I
take a sip of coffee or eat an apple than I make a mad dash
for my toothpaste, waging war against "noxious sulfide
gases" and bacteria that television commercials depict as
full-fledged monsters gnashing razor-sharp incisors until
they are swept away on an antiseptic tidal wave, leaving
one's breath "fresh, clean, and kissing sweet."

One specific type of dirt I not only tolerate but am actually proud of: the ink stains that appear on my right hand
after a hard day's work rubbing it across the pages of my
manuscripts. I take a great deal of satisfaction in examining myself for black splotches, which provide a symbolic
testament to my labor, much as the dirt on a farmer's over-
alls provides visual confirmation of *his* industriousness,
the blood, sweat, and tears that rarely soil the neat white
shirts and smartly tailored suits of the white-collar worker. The loss of visible evidence of our jobs on our clothing

has, in a subtle way, diminished us psychologically, accustomed as we once were to seeing on our pants and shoes the traces of the Protestant work ethic, which has been eliminated from our laundry by bleaches and "whiteners." My own means of counteracting the damaging emotional consequences of stainlessness is to maintain one emblematic spot of dirt where the Protestant work ethic clashes with the new cult of cleanness. This tiny protest against the tyranny of the immaculate is entirely disingenuous, however, since I would never take a job that truly compromised my hygiene, that left me covered in ink stains like a compositor or reeking of the odors of food, but am content to gaze admiringly at a single, circumscribed spot that satisfies my need to display to others, as well as to myself, clear signs of hard work.

The artful dishevelment of my wardrobe, which I discussed in "Dressing," is a way of resisting another monster that haunts my hygienic fantasy life, the unsavory figure of the overcoiffed queen, his face freshly moisturized, his cheeks lightly tanned with bronzer, his hair cemented in place with gobs of setting gel. Flouting the fastidious grooming of conventional gay men, I have radically simplified my own hygienic rituals and even indulge in such manly affectations as shaving with soap instead of shaving cream and cutting my own hair with dull electric sheers that leave in their wake broad swathes of bare scalp and tufts of split ends that spring upright no matter how much water I use to plaster them back down. In one key respect, however, I subscribe to the fussy habits of my kind: I con-

stantly trim the hairs from my nostrils, ears, and eyebrows, graying bristles that, now that I am over forty and
am producing higher levels of testosterone, are sprouting
up everywhere, even on my back and shoulders, destroying my boyish skin. It is not as if I am unusually preoccupied with becoming old: I am preoccupied with becoming
an old *male*, a hoary, ursine creature that can no longer
credibly play the part of the beardless puppy, the winsome
sapling who arouses the lust of older men. When women
age, they too must relinquish their girlishness but they are
never expected to change their sexual roles in bed, whereas aging gay men are expected to abandon the pleasures
of their passivity and become the chaser, not the chased,
the grizzled pederast who trips all over himself in order to
secure the affections of the ephebe, the smooth-chinned
Patroclus, who, in my heart of hearts, I still want to be
even at the age of forty-three, despite my owlish eyebrows
and the silvery fleece spreading over my chest.

Even my toenails are turning into horny yellow talons.
I find this problem less distressing than my unwanted hair
because I bite them down to the quick with my teeth.
Gifted with double-jointed legs, both of which I was once
able to wrap around the back of my neck at the same time
like a contortionist, I have eaten my toenails, as well as my
fingernails, since childhood, foregoing clippers and emery
boards for the convenience of my powerful jaws. As hard
as I have struggled to control this bad habit, I am constantly tearing off tiny slivers of flesh and bleeding all over
my books and drafts. Gnawing on my fingers and toes, I

am also declawing myself, removing from my body appendages that were once essential tools, weapons of self-defense, vitally important in fending off predators and ripping into food but that, after we have conquered our environments with hammers and screwdrivers, are now completely useless. Like cats, we are thoroughly domesticated animals, suited for indoor living, and as a result we can afford to engage in these self-inflicted manicures that testify, not only to the absence of physical danger in our lives, but to the increasing automation of a push-button world in which machines have triumphed over the human body. Whereas I myself engage in gymnastic pedicures, others demonstrate the uselessness of their nails by beautifying them, by spending hours in expensive salons softening their cuticles in finger bowls and painting their nails shocking shades of emerald and scarlet, narcissistic routines that show how the aesthetics of hands and feet have superseded their utility.

My savage grooming is not so much a routine of self-maintenance as a method of self-investigation, much as children explore their worlds by sticking things into their mouths, attempting to acquire knowledge in the same way that Eve did in the Garden of Eden, by incorporating marbles and dolls into their bodies, as if by absorbing them, by making them a part of themselves, they would understand them. Biting my toenails, eating my scabs, and swallowing dead skin clipped from the calluses on my hands and the soles of my feet are final vestiges of this technique of infantile empirical investigation. This crude form of oral self-education has lingered on among adults as one of the sole remaining avenues for rediscovering ourselves in an age that has transformed our bodies into uncharted regions that we long to inspect, biting every nail, smelling every fart, and examining every turd and drop of piss, which are no sooner released than they are flushed from sight, leaving us strangers to our own productions.

9

Cleaning and Decorating

If children learn to pick up after themselves by example, I was the victim of an execrable, if well-meaning, role model, my loving mother, who, on the infrequent occasions that she gave our house a thorough cleaning, shoved everything behind the sofa and into junk drawers and dragged around in her wake an enormous plastic garbage bag into which she emptied dozens of overflowing ash trays and a month's worth of used Kleenexes and yellowing newspapers. She was so negligent in her duties as a housewife that I once told her I was going to buy her a long stick with a sharp metal spike so that she could patrol the house like the custodian of a public park, skewering the debris strewn in her path without bending over to pick it up.

A MEMOIR OF NO ONE IN PARTICULAR

It was at least in part because of Mother's habitual neglect of her housekeeping duties that I have been an incorrigible slob for the better part of my life, especially during my childhood, when my room was cluttered with cast-off clothing, undressed dolls, overturned game boards, unfinished puzzles, and piles of brightly colored wooden blocks. Tidying up was torture for me as a child because it was linked to the cessation of play, to the tedium of ordinary living, an association that still contributes to the unpleasantness of an activity that I neglected well into my thirties, playing blocks with my books, shoes, and clothing long after my last toy had been carted off to the attic. We make our debuts as house cleaners by putting away Hot Wheels, Barbies, and Tonka Toy trucks, establishing, almost in infancy, a causal connection between straightening our rooms and the unwelcome interruption of recreational activities whose abrupt end provokes shrieking tantrums in ill-behaved children.

Books, not blocks, are now the biggest source of clutter in my apartment. They are also my chief form of decoration. Although I consult my bookshelves frequently, I have amassed my library, as any candid reader will tell you, primarily for show, much as old-fashioned housewives accumulate in their hutches linen tablecloths, napkin rings, silver platters, tea sets, and china for the dinner parties that, on the few occasions they occur, serve as public demonstrations of a hostess's talents as an entertainer. The ten six-foot-high cases of my library, holding roughly fifteen hundred books, the majority crumbling paperbacks, are the equivalent of the dining room hutch, a depository in which I proudly display for my visitors the tools of my trade: a compact *OED* that I haven't touched in at least three years, a complete set of Hawthorne, and well over one hundred black Penguin classics. Unlike plumbers, who keep their wrenches and plungers in their bags, or carpenters, who keep their lathes and drill presses in their shops, intellectuals are among the only workers who actually incorporate their tools into their interior decoration. Lined with moth-eaten tomes, these vast wooden monuments seldom amount to much more than pyramids of paste and paper in which we inter a social role as archaic as that of the chatelaine and the hostess: the reader. One of the reasons that I feel such a strong need to show off my scholarly equipment is that I am showing off a form of power and prestige that intellectuals no longer have, uncertain as we are about our value in a society whose living rooms are crowded not with book shelves but with "entertainment centers." Our libraries are in fact the mausoleums of neglected megalomaniacs who assert the control they feel they are losing through the ineffectual, if psychologically reassuring, method of advertising their intellectual wealth aesthetically, just as the nouveaux riches wear expensive jewelry and drive around in fancy cars.

If I have allowed my books to become dust farms, I am much more strict with myself about one particular aspect of my apartment, my floors, which I continually sweep, chasing elusive dust bunnies that dart impishly away from the angry stabs I make with my broom. Like most people, I adhere to the strictures of an irrational floor taboo and avoid contact with it as much as possible, throwing out food that I accidentally drop, wearing socks or slippers at all times, and preventing blankets and clothing from trailing across a region I view as a source of contagion, contaminated by the soles of our shoes, which track in dirt and excrement from the outside world. In the 1960s and 1970s, I experienced a temporary suspension of the floor taboo and returned to it much as members of the counterculture returned to nature, an entity with which my mother's green and orange shag rug carpets in some sense became synonymous, the synthetic surfaces on which noble savages in sandals and tie-dyed T-shirts unfurled their futons and sat cross-legged, smoking pot. Our daily sit-ins with our friends in our bedrooms were anti-Establishmentarian seances in which we regressed to an aboriginal state, that of suburban primitives who rejected furniture, in all of its complacent coziness, as a way of turning our backs on a corrupt civilization and the overupholstered appurtenances for which our house-proud parents scrimped and saved.

Only in my thirties did I manage to reelevate myself, to transcend the floor, which once again became dark and drafty, an abyss over which I am suspended like a cliff dweller, the owner of a real bed and a real table (whose legs are equipped with lions' feet to scare away the demons that scurry around the wainscoting). For me, becoming an adult involved a literal form of ascension in which I rejected the crouching postures of the hippy. In giving up the cushion for the chair, I relived an abbreviated version of evolutionary history. Perhaps our culture's floor taboo is an homage to keeping upright, to being a biped, to having abandoned our lowly, simian lives when we crawled around as quadrupeds on the ultimate floor, the grassy prairie, whereas we now float daintily above it, dangling in our hammocks and kicking our legs over the edges of our chairs, unwilling to set our dainty paws in the muck.

My disgust with the floor is intensified by one of the major obstacles my broom encounters: extension cords. We are constantly pulling at cords, tugging on them to make them stretch farther, inadvertently unplugging our vacuum sweepers as we plunge them into inaccessible corners, wrestling with the fact that our machines are tethered to their outlets, anchored in surge-protector strips and shackled on uncomfortably short leashes. Yanking cords is one of the pathologies of indoor living and a major source of irritation with our machines, which impose on us their own immobility, as was once the case with our telephones, which moored us to their jacks until portables liberated us from braided cables that invariably wound themselves in tangled bows and inextricable loops. In most respects, life indoors was far more constricted in the preindustrial era, when people were forced to huddle around their stoves and lanterns for heat and light, but the Machine Age has created its own forms of imprisonment, which have complicated the psychology of the house and inspired frustrations that make us long to pull the plug on a world crowded with unnecessary electronic devices. We experience the ultimate form of appliance bondage with our television sets and PCs, which have contributed to our inactivity and destroyed our waistlines.

If I never lose consciousness of my floors, I have lost sight entirely of my walls, which have all but disappeared from my field of vision, despite the fact that they are lined with my intricate doodles—grotesque framed fantasies of vagina dentatas in party dresses and epicene chimeras with breasts and full erections. Everything I put on my walls eventually disappears, merging into a gestalt that creates, for purposes of indoor living alone, a type of perception quite distinct from that which we use out-of-doors, where the unpredictability of obstacles in our paths—fast-moving cars, potholes, messengers careening around corners on mountain bikes—keeps us constantly on guard. When we are in our houses, by contrast, we do not need to be as alert and therefore seldom perceive our possessions as individual objects with a distinct, autonomous presence but only as dim, shadowy forms that exist solely in their relations to each other, as part of a complex matrix of connections, my alarm clock always residing next to my bedside water glass, my radio next to my oval lamp, my Boston fern next to my armchair next to my battered coffee table with the fake Favril vase full of dried roses.

Only when these links are disturbed, when I buy a jarring new Indian bedspread, move my cactus from one side of the room to another, or even change the wattage of the bulb in my desk lamp, do I truly see the furnishings in my apartment as something separate from me rather than just immaterial props on an internal stage. The act of house-cleaning, in fact, is about the maintenance and preservation of the gestalt, about restoring our obliviousness to the external world, a type of habituation that is integral to our very idea of comfort, of coziness. Relaxing indoors involves a significant reduction in attentiveness, a much-needed reprieve from the high degree of vigilance we maintain out on the streets, where we must avoid running into utility poles, stepping into piles of dogshit, or wading ankle-deep through flooded storm sewers. When I pick up my rooms, I am recreating preestablished relations between things, sharpening connections that have been blurred by clutter, eliminating objects that interfere with these links and thus compromise the gestalt. I find messiness so psychologically uncomfortable, not only because of guilt, but because it is the most philosophical state, its complexity preventing me from taking my environment for granted, from ceasing to think about it. Mess makes me concentrate too much, forces me to *see* my rooms, which, once they become too disordered to be taken for granted, I immediately clean in order to alleviate the inconvenience of potential obstructions I long to sub-merge in the reassuring void of the gestalt, thereby keep-ing my house snug and homey.

Although I seldom dust, I am thoroughly repelled by the thin film that lies over everything in my rooms, the powdery accumulation of a particle storm that has no clear source of origin, no clouds, but that nonetheless keeps mysteriously streaming down, no matter how often I perform the essentially meaningless task of wiping every surface in my apartment. Dust is an iconic form of dirt in a capitalist society, not because agricultural communities didn't have to contend with it, but because conspicuous consumption burdens us with possessions that are never used and hence lie undisturbed, ignored on coffee tables and whatnot shelves, coated in a mantle of fibrous fuzz. When people owned fewer things and regularly used those they acquired, their belongings were constantly being moved and hence did not simply sit stock-still, passively accepting the slow-motion shower of bits of dirt and threads sloughed from textiles drifting down upon them like invisible confetti. Desuetude is the housecleaning malaise of the modern dwelling, which gets dirty not because it is in use but because it is so thoroughly *out of use*, unoccupied during the day for long periods of time and, for the most part, idle even when its residents are at home, busily striding through rooms whose contents, like those in museum cases, are rarely seen, let alone touched.

My aesthetic of interior decoration is based on a model that is intrinsically prone to dust: the still life. I am always trying to turn my rooms into static compositions, symmetrical arrangements of exquisite objects, of thick-glass bottles filled with pussy willow branches and sprigs of dried flowers, brightly colored bedspreads, curiously woven wicker baskets, and lush ivy vines and ferns that hang in my windows suspended from invisible plastic threads.

Unfortunately, two things undermine the cryptlike paralysis of this studiedly tasteful art installation, this site-specific *nature morte*: only statues live in still lifes and I am decidedly *not* a statue but a large and somewhat oafish man who leaves in his wake used Kleenexes, dirty coffee cups, dictionaries, and ballpoint pens with caps dinted with tooth marks; what's more, the aesthetic of motion-lessness is founded on a lie of closure antithetical to consumerism, since most people treat their houses as forever unfinished projects in which they are always putzing, rearranging their furniture, repainting their walls, and laying down new carpets. The rooms of an acquisitive culture are always in motion, always evolving, mutating into brand-new forms, their contents multiplying, proliferating on every counter and shelf, despite the illusion we fabricate of the morguelike permanence of our houses, the marmoreal repose of a necropolis whose presumably deceased inhabitants remain conveniently still. Dead men alone are capable of residing comfortably in the midst of this cold, unfriendly elegance, ghosts who never disturb the furnishings of the castles they haunt.

The fact that a beautiful interior is not necessarily a habitable one can be seen in the case of my desk, one of the most psychologically disturbed places in my apartment, a plank of polyurethaned pine on which aesthetics and utility wage war, facing off on fifteen square feet. Some of my most intense housecleaning conflicts take place on this battle-fatigued surface, where my need for prettiness clashes with my need to fan out my papers, flip

– 177 –

through half a dozen open books, and scatter around sheets of rejected drafts. Every night, I perform penance for all those years my parents stumbled over my blocks and carefully return my manuscripts to a straw box, place my dictionary in its drawer, put away stacks of dog-eared notebooks, and smooth the wrinkles out of the red strip of cloth on which I keep my laptop. And yet no matter how conscientiously I strive to keep my desk immaculate, it always reverts to its natural state of squalor. The look of pristine uselessness is ruined in a matter of weeks, and the beautiful still life becomes a messy workshop in which my pens, diskettes, and legal pads are abandoned where they were last used. The narrative pattern of my housecleaning, of order followed inevitably by chaos, suggests that aesthetics and utility are often at odds, that beauty is inconvenient, that it inhibits movement, thwarts our efforts to work in our environments, and creates a level of inanimateness, of deadness, incompatible with the very state of being alive.

My concept of beauty is so disdainful of the worker and his physical needs that there are only two pieces of upholstered furniture in my apartment, my desk chair and my recliner, a *faux* Queen Anne which, out of necessity, sacrifices aesthetics to comfort, since I lie in it virtually supine for the better part of my waking hours. Everything else I own is made of wood, a substance that represents for me a supercilious rejection of the overupholstered look of my childhood, and my parents' need to eliminate angles and corners from their lives, to soft-sculpturize their environments, and buy furnishings from materials that are increasingly like our own bodies, smooth and pliable. I follow instead the aesthetic of the hard edge, the sharp contour, a high-brow look based on my contempt for the creature comforts of the bourgeois, for coziness, which has turned everything we own into one big cushion. My notion of elegance is bound up with the look of discomfort, of the *uncozy*, a look central to modernism and the white cube, with its purgatorial chairs that force us to sit ramrod straight, vacant walls, cold wood floors stripped of plush carpets, and sofas as snug and commodious as assemblages by Archipenko. Evoking the minimalist idiom of the classic avant garde, I have adopted an antiphysical style of interior decoration. This self-punishing austerity challenges the complacency of the typical middle American household, whose rooms, filled with overstuffed armchairs, swollen ottomans, and wall-to-wall shag rugs, express a distinctly bovine and self-satisfied philosophy of life. Like so much modern architecture, the *nature morte* I have created for myself excludes the body, erases the occupant, and administers tasteful doses of discomfort in order to register a subtle, snobbish protest against those who have designed their rooms like pillows that caress their plump derrieres and tumescent bellies.

I once wrote an essay in which I contrasted two styles of interior decoration by describing the differences between my mother's living room in Asheville, North Carolina, and Cher's in Malibu: in the first, the room functions as the three-dimensional life story of its principal occupant, an archive of keepsakes, family photographs, and souvenirs from past vacations; and in the second, the room expresses a far more impersonal aesthetic, one that, in the case of the well-to-do, is often not even the occupant's own but a costly mercenary's, her designer's, and that can be changed at will, just as Cher redecorates her house every sixteen months, her faux Egyptian sphinxes and wingèd scarabs giving way to Cherokee chevrons and tasteful Navajo throw rugs. Mother's living room, by contrast, is a lifelong work-in-progress that changes only gradually through accumulation, not through the arbitrary fiat of a designer who creates houses that are mere physical extensions of the owner's infinitely plastic sense of self, of his belief in his unfettered individuality, his ability to invent, through interior design, an entirely new identity. Mother's room is about remembering, Cher's, about forgetting, about the liberating release of selective architectural amnesia, about starting life all over again in brand-new rooms, which sever the very connection with the past that Mother is so anxious to preserve.

Within this scheme, my own apartment is, regrettably, more like Cher's than my mother's. Everything I own, with the exception of my library, is no more than five years old, from my Teflon skillets to my cordless phones, from my wicker clothes hamper to the solid glass bricks I use as bookends. I have made a fundamental break with my past, a rupture embodied in my decor, which bears no trace of my history, no aging daguerreotypes of great-grandparents or of the old family homestead. The aesthetic of "no one in particular" is, at best, one of generic elegance. The curious absence of memorabilia everywhere you look in my two rooms expresses my often oppressive sense that I am a man without a past, someone who created his life exactly as he designed his environment, according to his own plan, his own blueprint.

10

Lying

The most sadistic homework assignment I ever received was given by my English teacher in a working-class elementary school in Tanawanda, New York, where I lived briefly between the ages of nine and ten. She told us to read a novel of our choice, make a five-minute oral report in which we were to persuade our classmates to read the book, and then stand at our desks, our pleading eyes roaming the room, while votes were tallied about how convincing we had been. My best friend was an orthodox Jew with a bulbous nose and two yellowing tusks for front teeth. He approached the assignment in a way that unfortunately exceeded his meager theatrical talents: he jammed a stovepipe hat made of black construction paper over his yarmulke and, in a whimpering, high-pitched British accent, pretended he was Dr. Doolittle himself introducing us, creature by creature, to the enchanting menagerie featured in his book.

He was, of course, greeted by snickers and then by a silence as cruel as a stoning in a public square. Not a single person voted in his favor, but a flurry of hands shot up the second our instructor asked if they would rather read *The Isle of the Blue Dolphins*, on the basis of Jim's succinct and lively report, or *Charlotte's Web*, on the basis of Mary's clearly sincere expression of sorrow for aging arachnids. That evening, while recapping the day's events for my mother, I mentioned the episode in passing and showed no guilt whatsoever about buckling under peer pressure and refusing to support my friend in his hour of need. Although she was generally soft-spoken with her children and listened politely as I prattled on about my day, this time her temper flared and she raised her voice to utter, with rabbinical severity, what was to become for me the Eleventh Commandment: "WE LIE! WE LIE FOR OUR FRIENDS!"

Unlike other children, who were weaned on the legends of George Washington and his cherry tree and Honest Abe hiking miles to return a penny that someone had given him by mistake, I was taught the morality, the decency, the kindness, of strategic acts of deceit and dishonesty. Years later, I myself was the lucky beneficiary of a compassionate lie during a marital mishap with my first lover, Anthony, who inadvertently groped my friend Randy in the darkness of a cruise park, mistaking him for a mysterious stranger until their lips were just about to meet. Anthony made Randy swear not to tell me about these clumsy overtures but, doubting his word, decided instead to slink home and make a clean breast of it. Some demon deep within me made me call Randy the next day and begin rhapsodizing about Anthony's loyalty, about my implicit trust of him, about the infidelity of other boyfriends in contrast to the devotion of my own beloved companion—praise that Randy greeted with an unenthusiastic series of "uh-huh" 's and "oh yes" 's. Never once during this diabolical temptation did he waver and break the Eleventh Commandment. I was forced to admit defeat in my test of his honor and congratulate him on his high-minded duplicity, whereupon we burst into laughter and relived the mortifying moonlit scene.

A world without tact would be both inhuman and infinitely more complicated. Lying saves time, is emotionally economical, and streamlines human interactions by substituting pat, incontestable alibis for murky, refutable ones, as when I explained to a friend that I could not attend her dinner party because I had a "prior engagement" when the fact of the matter is that I detest her husband, a reason that would not only have hurt her feelings but embroiled me in a lengthy and unprofitable argument, much to the detriment of that day's writing schedule. Honesty is seldom, if ever, the best policy. A perfect stranger with whom I had had a single sexual encounter once waylaid me on the street and insisted on knowing why I hadn't called him, deploring my unwillingness to be straightforward and badgering me about being "incapable of intimacy," "emotionally dishonest," and not "true to your feelings," as if our torrid love affair had lasted for twenty-five years rather than twenty-five minutes. Exasperated by his self-serving denunciations, I finally flew off the handle and blurted out what he clearly did not expect, the truth: that I did not wish to see him because I found him fat, old, and ugly, a criticism that, while below the belt, he surely deserved but that led to an "incident" on the sidewalk in the course of which he raised his voice and jabbed me in the chest with his index finger. It would perhaps have been better all around if I had ignored his criticisms and obeyed the Eleventh Commandment rather than giving him the one answer that, his protestations notwithstanding, he was clearly unprepared to hear.

If there is an art to lying, it is governed by a minimalist aesthetic. When I am forced to wriggle out of an invitation, I prefer to say that "I am too busy" or that I am "under the weather" rather than "I cannot come because I am accepting an award for life achievement in literature at the Algonquin Club" or "I would love to drop by but I must sit at home all evening by the telephone waiting for a call from the President who is trying to secure me a diplomatic post in Paris." In order to ensure credibility, most people's lies are extremely laconic and uninventive, not soaring flights of fancy in which they indulge in the pleasures of tall tales but curt formulae in which the narrative impulse to expand and embroider has been suppressed by guilt, the stupefyingly prosaic muse of the lie. As willingly as I do it, I despise perjuring myself so much that my fibs rarely amount to more than one or two words whose brevity serves a precise function. When I was a graduate student, an eccentric acquaintance of mine brought into the coffee shop we frequented an enormous sheaf of her watercolors, ghastly daubs of desiccated lemons and flabby peaches—a collection I was forced to admire while my friend Joaquin smirked in my peripheral vision. Stifling the urge to laugh, I made my way through the entire stack by choking out such noncommittal words of praise as "nice," "pretty," and "interesting"— panegyrics in her eyes, it would seem, since my terseness never registered as ambivalence or led her to put away this paradise of unearthly delights. Although it is by no means foolproof, the simplicity of my lies serves the utilitarian purpose of derailing an exchange I find uncomfortable, of expressing disengagement and thereby terminating the need for falsifications by making as perfunctory a contribution as possible to the conversation. My lies often rely on painful displays of incuriosity, which I intend to have a dampening effect on the encounter but which I am appalled to discover seldom discourage the undiscerning, who remain indifferent to the apparently illegible cues I use to silence them.

Only pathological liars lie in a discursive and imaginative way, intoxicated with the thrill of leading an alternative life, as in the case of a man I knew in Boston who, pulling the wool over the eyes of even his closest friends, mastered both the accent and the idiom of an Australian and created for himself an imaginary past as a picaresque expatriate from Toowoomba. Most of us, however, have too strong an allegiance to our personalities, which we have painstakingly constructed over decades, to behave with the reckless abandon of such sociopathic chameleons, who demonstrate an almost Keatsian negative capability to assume any form, unconstrained by remorse about betraying their authentic self. Only as children and adolescents do we indulge in elaborate lies and then only because we have no past and the self is unformed. In the third grade, for instance, I perpetrated an unconscionable hoax. Because all of my friends were getting glasses, I set out to fail my annual eye exam but failed it so spectacularly that the school nurse concluded I was going blind and sent me to a local specialist, who, in turn, referred me to another specialist who referred me to another, until, months later, slipping into premature darkness at the age of eight, I ended up in the hands of an ophthalmologist skilled in the art of unmasking impostors like myself. He caught me giving inconsistent reactions to his tests and confronted me on the spot, saying "You're lying," whereupon I crumpled into a sobbing heap while he scolded me for the amount of money that had been wasted and for causing my parents such grief.

At first, all I wanted was glasses, but as the deception became more complex and my parents became increasingly alarmed, I began to enjoy being the victim of a mysterious disease, an invalid struck down before his prime by an exotic ailment that eluded the best efforts of an entire team of specialists. The lie was a way of inventing a personality for myself—in this instance, that of a dying Camille, a well-defined identity that I did not have but that would emerge only later after years of very different kinds of flimflams and impersonations, through a pastiche of my favorite authors, for instance, and an ever-changing dumb show of dramatic poses representing the suffering genius. In the absence of any more effective means of creating change, lies for me were ways of altering reality, rejections of the basic facts of my biography, techniques for expressing dissatisfaction with its tedium, for imagining another sort of existence altogether, a parallel personality that I could aspire to be. Had I not lied, had I not devised for myself the snobbish persona of a sophisticated aesthete marooned in Appalachia (a lie if there ever was one), I would never have become a writer, would have remained true to my upbringing, stayed in the South, received an inferior education, and developed into an altogether different sort of person. The ability to conceive of another life, another personality, through seemingly infantile fantasies is the very essence of ambition, of the motivation to change, and those who do not have the courage to practice this kind of negative capability accept their lot unquestioningly and never look for anything better, denying themselves the mobility that the liar creates by refusing to accept the truth, willing it away.

One major lie of my adolescence has had a deep impact, not only on my personality, but on my appearance. Beginning at the age of fourteen, when I fell in love with my high school history instructor, and ending in my late teens, when I was smitten with a romantic poet with a thick shock of raven-black hair and a deep Southern brogue that made me weak in my knees, I hid my burning passion for heterosexual men under a cool and collected affectation of platonic intimacy, all the while swooning away every time they rolled up a sleeve, showed an inch or two of hairy leg, or unbuttoned their shirt to expose their sun-tanned cleavage. Throughout these unrequited obsessions, I was filled with a sense of the moral untenability of my position as their confidant, of having secured their affections under false pretenses, concealing my real feelings, listening patiently to their girl troubles, and consoling them over their professional disappointments. The need to bluff my way through a series of crushes that, over time, became elaborate swindles, full of unspoken longings and fleeting, stolen touches, left me with a permanent sense of disgust for my hypocrisy. In part, I turned up the volume of my effeminacy to prevent myself from ever engaging in such covert schemes again, letting my voice and gestures serve as my own in-house tattletale, which continually outs me in spite of myself. I have made sure that my homosexuality is written into my body like a tattoo so that I can never innocently ensnare the affections of an unwitting straight man. In order to avoid the ordeal of coming out over and over again, I have made one emphatic *physical* declaration, a confession that, out of emotional laziness, relieves me of the responsibility of repeatedly telling the truth, since the truth tells itself in my gait and intonations, a style of self-presentation that allows me to be honest without spelling it out in so many words, to reveal my true colors without having to face the shock of open confessions.

I am most vulnerable to lying when I engage in story-telling for the amusement of others, whether I am recall-ing a confrontation that took place earlier in the day or an incident that occurred in the very distant past. When I was in graduate school, I used to tell a story that I have now retired from my repertoire because I am convinced that it is altogether implausible, even though its narrative structure is so compelling that it has entirely displaced all recollection of what really happened. It has become, for all intents and purposes, an implanted memory, like the microchips inserted into the brains of the unsuspecting androids in *Blade Runner*. I was sunbathing on my roof in Boston's Back Bay, wearing a bandana to protect my scalp from further damage by ultraviolet rays, and sitting with my back to the construction site of the new extension of the Ritz-Carlton, when I heard gruff, insistent voices calling out to me. I turned my head and saw a group of men in hard hats looking in my direction and yelling out something that I interpreted (possibly in retrospect) as "Show us your boobies." I concluded at the time (or, again, possibly in retrospect as the story was tailored for public consumption) that they had mistaken me for an immodest woman sunbathing without a top, and I began (or did I?) to flutter my hand over my shoulder as if to say, "Oh you silly brutes, stop it now!," working them up to a pitch of sexual excitement. They continued to request that I display my boobies, whereupon, after several more girlish protests and dismissive waves, I stood up, whipped off my bandana, shook it teasingly at them, and stuck out my flat chest as they groaned in unison at their mistake and rapidly dispersed throughout the building.

Did this incident even happen? I have told it so often that I do not in all honesty really know, but I am convinced that life is seldom so shapely and therefore detect the presence of a manipulating intelligence that gave a somewhat amorphous and inconclusive incident sharper narrative contours than it could possibly have had. Everything about this story smacks of vanity and serves to exalt me, an effeminate homosexual, over one of gay men's traditional enemies, the homophobic construction worker, who inadvertently engages in homoerotic behavior in the middle of his favorite heterosexual pastime, that of catcalling women in the streets. The anecdote seems to me a clear instance of bragging, of self-glorification, the primary reason that most of our stories are lies. We bore our friends with shameless celebrations of our courage, ingeniousness, and audacity, wish fulfillments in which we emerge triumphant, regardless of how—in reality—we fell flat on our faces, ducked and ran for cover while our opponents humiliated us.

I am much more certain of the distortions involved in another of my favorite anecdotes, my close brush with electroshock. When I came out to my parents at thirteen, my father—very forgivably influenced by Skinner and the behavioral modification movement fashionable among psychologists at the time—decided to introduce me to the glories of heterosexuality through a mild form of aversive shock therapy. He intended to attach electrodes to the sensitive skin of my forearms, hold up pictures of naked men and women, and then turn on the juice with the former while allowing me to appreciate in peace the beautiful, curvaceous forms of the latter, whose voluptuousness would be forever linked in my mind with the cessation of pain. I refused treatment, however, not because I had any moral objections to what most would consider a barbaric form of coercion, but because I was ashamed of looking at dirty photographs in front of my father. He was forced to drop the project and retire this nefarious instrument of torture to the closet, where it gathered dust until I brought it out to dazzle the scientific community with the startling discoveries I made in the course of my ninth-grade physics project. Over a period of weeks, I electrocuted a set of ivy plants (without even showing them dirty pictures) and eventually destroyed the shocker altogether but not before I won third place in the Western North Carolina Science Fair, even though my conclusions were less than flabbergasting, namely, that nothing whatsoever happens when you submit common creepers to aversive shock therapy, the exact same result that I suspect my father would have attained had he proceeded with his attempts to change my sexuality.

While the only explicit lie I make when I tell this story is that I won first prize (not third) in the statewide (not regional) science fair, I make a subtle ideological adjustment to the narrative that falsifies its meaning entirely. I pretend that I set out to destroy the shocker in a carefully planned act of revenge, that I was waging a vendetta against the tool of my oppression, that my scientific experiment was a just reprisal against a machine that embodied homophobia, when in fact the shocker met its demise simply through my carelessness and rough treatment. In other words, I superimpose on the story a self-aggrandizing shape, the flattering portrait of a budding gay liberationist who proudly asserts his sexual identity and outwits the schemes of his elders to force him to relinquish his secret longings.

Similar distortions occur in the story I tell about my mother's practical joke of greeting me suggestively in the doorway of her bedroom wearing a long blond wig, her mouth an obscene gash of bright-red lipstick. When I first introduced this anecdote into my repertoire, I told it somewhat differently, that she greeted me in the doorway, not only tarted up like a *fille de joie*, but entirely naked, which — scandalous as it may seem — is precisely how I remember her. In more recent versions of the story, however, I have modestly reclothed her, partly because I doubt my own veracity and feel that even someone as outlandish as my mother would not have done anything as shockingly oedipal as entice me into her bedroom in her birthday suit, and in part because the reactions of others to the ur-story were so ambivalent, eliciting at best embarrassed smiles at her satirical irreverence for motherhood. The lies that gave this story its final shape are twofold and contradictory. On the one hand, the narrative is another clear instance of bragging on the part of a son enormously proud of his mother's unconventionality, which he overstates at the risk of defaming her, and on the other, the story has been modified by social pressures, both by the prudery of my audience, which insists that I place a fig leaf over the narrative's naughty bits, and by my own desire to maintain plausibility, that fragile balance of verisimilitude and hyperbole so easily endangered by minute errors of judgment. Although her nudity may only be another implanted memory, the fact of the matter is that, in my mind's eye, I still see her there in the doorway stark naked, and it is thus possible that I am lying so that the truth will seem less startling and hence less false. Perhaps what really happened is, by an unfortunate coincidence, too similar to fiction to credit, a resemblance I downplay by subduing, not exaggerating, its seemingly make-believe improbability. Truth may be stranger than fiction, but in order to tell good stories, one must pretend that it is never so.

I am also very susceptible to lying when I engage in storytelling because I simply do not remember everything that happened in the past but am unwilling to present to others narratives that, were I to adhere scrupulously to the facts, would be riddled with gaping holes that would destroy their effectiveness as entertainment. I do not remember, for instance, whether the would-be Aussie in Boston claimed to be from Toowoomba, nor do I remember the exact words of the aspersions my spurned suitor cast on me, nor do I remember the titles of the literary works on which Mary and Jim delivered their exemplary book reports, nor, for that matter, do I remember their names, "Mary" and "Jim." Rather than giving my audience a mass of broken fragments, I guiltlessly supply reasonable transitions and fiddle with faults of logic in order to create a smooth, flowing seamlessness that daily experience, in its purest and most immediate form, rarely has. Stories are epistemological experiments in which we take the recalcitrant material of the things that happen to us and sculpt them into recognizable shapes rather than merely itemize them in laundry lists of chance incidents, as happens when unintelligent people describe, in a tedious fashion, what occurred during the course of a day, unable to subordinate one event to another, to create hierarchies of the important and the trivial, to use to their advantage the organizing force of narrative.

I tell stories not only to entertain but also to illustrate, to buttress my arguments, to provide an ersatz form of evidence, as writers and orators have done throughout history, from the bowdlerized stories drawn from Ovid's *Metamorphoses* and used in highly sanitized versions in the sermons of medieval preachers to the feel-good human-interest anecdotes told by politicians stumping on the campaign trail about unwed crack heads with ten HIV-positive children who miraculously kick their habits and work their way off welfare. I too lie for the sake of shoring up the points I make, as in the case of the story I tell in "Laughing" about stepping up on the desk and singing

"Climb Every Mountain," an incident that did indeed occur but with one major difference: my aria was not interrupted by a partner entering the room. What remains true about this story is that I cease joking, often midsentence, the instant anyone more powerful than myself comes into the word-processing center. The interruptions are seldom as dramatic, however, as being caught performing a Rogers and Hammerstein musical on top of my desk but usually occur at subtler moments that don't lend themselves to entertaining descriptions, as when I tease my colleagues about their chemical addictions or their rampant promiscuity, occasions in which I simply shut up if a lawyer walks in the middle of my act.

My nose grows by exactly 1.9 centimeters at one crucial moment, when I cite numbers, which are subject to wild and irresponsible exaggerations, their decimal points careening from left to right at my convenience, the figures acquiring and shedding digits at will. A society of number crunchers worships its integers like deranged numerologists who invest all of the mathematical apparatus of their lives—their bank codes, social security numbers, cholesterol counts—with ineffable poetic and spiritual significance. Numeric lying is the easiest and least imaginative, if one of the most powerful, forms of exaggeration because it allows the uninventive liar to exploit his listeners' obsessions and alter reality significantly by uttering a single word that acts like a magician's incantation. Without fail, figures pulled from a hat mesmerize the modern audience, which eagerly rises to the bait of inflated calculations and staggering sums of cash. The very standard of truth in our culture, the all-mighty number, is trapped in a web of endless distortions. Statistics become a constant source of fibbing in a highly secular society in which quantity and cost are subject to the same sort of mythologizing that religious miracles once were, with legends of Bill Gates's salary or the value of Cher's Malibu mansion having the same otherworldly power as the appearance of the Virgin Mary or the Man of Sorrows on a rusty roadside billboard.

I also lie like a trooper on the numerous occasions I make ill-advised ventures into the world of science and politics, subjects that are now the exclusive province of experts and talking heads who spout facts and statistics that are always enviably at their fingertips. These mage-like figures have acquired so much glamour in the media that I, too, in all of my ignorance, attempt to arrogate to myself their authority and omniscience. When I explain to others the intricacies of angioplasties, rents in the ozone layer, carpal tunnel syndrome, and the beneficial effects of monoxide inhibitors, I become a freewheeling and irre-sponsible disseminator of misinformation, so entirely under the spell of the pundits who pontificate on talk shows and news hours that I mimic their infallibility. I know I am skating on thin ice whenever I use an alarm bell for lies, the expression "they say," a phrase that recurs in contemporary conversation (the "they" referring to those mysterious savants ensconced in their think tanks who awe the uninformed with their erudition).

A type of lie that is unique to recent history is what might be called the service-economy lie, the lies we make to corporations. We have no qualms about deceiving conglomerates in part because we do not feel that they are moral entities and also because we have been indoctrinated to believe that "the customer is always right," a permissive axiom of mom-and-pop capitalism that few Fortune 500 CEOs actually observe. When I destroyed my laptop computer late one drunken evening, I told the company that it was not my elbow but my cat (which I've never owned) that jostled the glass of water (in fact a syrupy concoction of rotgut vodka and Gatorade) that splashed a droplet (a torrent, a cataract, a tidal wave) into the keyboard, displacing responsibility onto a phantasmal tabby that haunts my desk, reeling into vases of flowers and trampling over sensitive electronic equipment. The lies we make to companies are assays into the stony heart of corporate America to determine whether there is anything even remotely resembling a thinking, feeling individual behind the bubbly voices of customer service representatives and twenty-four-hour support technicians who yes us to death even as we damn them to the ninth circle of hell for their obstinacy and unhelpfulness. Our ruses to get more (and better) service faster (and cheaper) are the protests the mass consumer registers against anonymity, an attempt to achieve personal contact with these indomitable abstractions by begging for special attention, by cutting in front of the line, by asking to be coddled as something more just than another faceless statistic but a real person with a very specific problem that must be redressed by someone compassionate enough to understand that ours is a peculiar case that defies the established rules.

All too frequently, I lie because I am not allowed to tell the truth. The two primary reasons that I avoid social engagements are, most important, that I would prefer to spend the time alone reading and, second, that my pockets are not deep enough to defray the costs of the extravaganzas that my more affluent friends think nothing of proposing, unaware that that junket to the Hamptons or that banquet at Le Cirque 2000 would consume, in one fell swoop, half of my monthly budget. In a society in which it is difficult to imagine that solitude is a real need, the excuse that one wants to be alone is misconstrued in two ways: as an unceremonious rebuff of the person who extends the invitation, and as a plea to be coaxed, to be begged to attend festivities that in fact fill one with dread, a cat-and-mouse game that most people willingly play for their friends, stroking their egos by insisting that their presence is mandatory. Likewise, to refuse invitations on the grounds that we are too poor is to open ourselves up to accusations that we are tightwads who abuse our friends' generous invitations to treat us to dinner and the movies, an allegation that all too frequently contains a grain of truth, the depth of our professed impecuniousness being in itself a small white lie. Neither the need for solitude nor the uncertain state of our finances is deemed an adequate justification for weaseling out of social obligations, and hence, in order to spare our purse and our pride, we keep on hand a recyclable stockpile of such expressions as "I'm busy, tired, booked, going away, attending a funeral, nursing a sick child, and celebrating my twenty-fifth wedding anniversary."

I lie most, however, when I do not lie at all. My life is divided between active lies — deliberate falsehoods that I use only as a last resort — and passive lies, lies of omission, lies that involve concealing my true opinions, effacing myself, retreating into my internal sanctuary, all the while nodding mechanically in polite agreement. I remain expressionless when my downstairs neighbor tells me about her new Suzanne Somers diet, which permits the consumption of slabs of bacon; when a colleague at work tells me about her rare gift of extrasensory perception and clairvoyance; when the host of a party praises an author I consider beneath contempt; or when an unstable woman of my acquaintance, unwilling to accept her fate as an old maid, damns the emotional immaturity of the opposite sex as the sole cause of her personal problems. I am overwhelmed by a stronger sense of dishonesty than most because I have spent my entire life as a somewhat jaundiced observer of my society and have taken great pains to develop my skills in detecting hypocrisy and lampooning the general idiocy of both myself and my fellow man.

And yet, as my mother's Eleventh Commandment reveals, a key part of my moral education was the necessity of being at all times courteous and empathetic, characteristics that make the life of a social critic a hard row to hoe. My work as a writer has put me into situations in which concealing what I feel is essential to both my social survival and my professional success, as when I investigated the way the Scientologists promoted their books and was forced to adopt a falsely congenial manner with a sinister group of high church ecclesiastics posing as a literary agency in Los Angeles called Authors' Services, something of a misnomer for an organization that represents a single author, L. Ron Hubbard. More recently, I wrote an essay on electronic cemeteries on the Internet where disconsolate "parents" post obituaries of their dead pets, from Chichi the Chihuahua, who overdosed on antifreeze, to Marshmallow the malamute, who suffered a fatal head injury after being dragged down the street by a car muffler. To my horror, soon after starting therapy, I spotted on my doctor's desk a book that pictured him embracing two enormous cocker spaniels, a guide to animal "grief management" that, after my heartless piece on the subject, induced a wave of panic and made me feel as if I had to leave the room that very instant at the risk of jeopardizing my already fragile mental health. Typically, I never mentioned the matter to my therapist, who was, as it turned out, perfectly competent, but let it fester, much to the detriment of our relationship, which was forever poisoned by my unvoiced realization that his practice was mired in the gimmicks of the self-help movement.

The conflict of my moral education and my responsibilities as a polemicist have forced me to lead a double life in which Dr. Jekyll dispenses a generous supply of benign

and supportive smiles while a smirking Mr. Hyde formu-
lates his opinions in secret. My inner dialogue is deafen-
ing, consisting of the running commentary of a backseat
driver jabbering away about the things that happen
around me, a blow-by-blow account that resembles the
breathless spiel of a sportscaster at a game or the rant of a
voluble fool at the movies who insists on narrating the
action on the screen as it occurs. My need to lie, to hold
my responses in check, to suppress my true feelings, has
resulted in a rich internal life, which is internal for one
very good reason: I have hidden it. If repression is the origin of the unconscious, of that repository of psychic
injuries too traumatic to withstand the light of day, lying
may be the origin of one's *conscious* life, one's awareness of
the border dividing one's public self from one's private
reflections. Subjectivity may have been created during the
primordial lie, at the very moment that one became aware
of the existence of an irreconcilable discrepancy with the
outside world, a conflict that led one to talk to oneself, to
mutter one's opinions like a madman in the soundproof
room of one's mind.

There are cracks in the acoustic tiling, however, and a
distant echo of my inner grouch can be heard in the language of my face and body, despite my efforts to dampen
the sound of the whines and squawks I keep muffled within. Hiding my opinions strains all of my physical resources
and causes an almost muscular fatigue from my exertions
to keep my facial expressions from disclosing my true feelings. As an undergraduate, I took a class on Romantic

poetry, which I disliked because my professor relied on unstructured discussions in which bewildered students, completely stumped by the insane prolixity of *Prometheus Unbound* or *The Book of Urizen*, tried valiantly, if never successfully, to sound smart. My instructor became so conscious of my disapproval of his Socratic methods that, even when he was writing on the blackboard, he would whip around, as if he felt my eyes boring holes into his back, and ask me what I wanted, convinced that I had raised my hand to pose a question when in fact I hadn't moved a finger. He began to call on me obsessively five or six times during every session until I was forced to sit at my desk as immobile as a cigar-store Indian. Even when I play dead, my body often tells the truth. A former boyfriend was fond of pointing out to me how brittle and fake my smiles looked, more like grimaces than grins, the result of the fact that the part of the brain that controls the muscles of the heartfelt smile, the so-called zygomatic smile, is not subject to conscious manipulation. We are not equipped, evolutionarily speaking, to lie. Other species can camouflage themselves from predators, changing their pigmentation at will and blending into the foliage, but human beings must live without protective coloration, at the mercy of the discerning eyes of their enemies.

It is not only my body that betrays me. I betray myself. I do not keep my views safely clapped up in the prison of my evil thoughts. I find myself incapable of being discreet and often feel as if I will explode from the pressure of the seething contents of my mind. I have therefore invented a faithful confidant, a gossip to whom I blab all of my unpleasant observations: the blank white page. Writing for me is a form of talking behind people's backs, of telling tales out of school, of relieving myself of the powerful sense of mendacity that haunts my interactions with others. It is because I lie to people's faces that I try so hard to tell the truth in my prose. Only a Phrygian barber knew that Apollo had awarded Midas a pair of ass's ears for his bad taste in music, a secret that the ill-fated king kept neatly tucked under a pointed dunce cap. Dying to reveal to others this scandalous deformity, the barber dug a hole in the ground and whispered it into the earth, but the nearby reeds heard him and began repeating the news among themselves until the entire kingdom knew the truth. My prose is the hole in which I confess the lies that I have told; my readers are the reeds that spread my dirty little secrets.

11

Reading

As a child, I was fascinated by one book in particular in my father's library, a slender black volume that stood out among forbidding texts on autism, schizophrenia, mental retardation, hyperactivity, alcoholism, and aberrant sexual behavior: *Paradise Lost*. It was the only book of poetry in his collection and he kept it as a frayed and mildewed relic of a class he had taken as an undergraduate, a whimsical elective that, having fulfilled all of the requirements for his degree, he enrolled in more or less as a lark. Its pages bore the scars of the heroic if unsuccessful battle that this single-mindedly pragmatic student had waged in the face of the unfamiliarity and seeming uselessness of literature. Approaching the project with the same rigor he brought to his study of statistics and abnormal child development, he covered the margins with annotations and, in a virtually illegible scrawl, glossed every line with its own translation, an interlinear paraphrase that explained Milton's syntax, allusions, and theology, so incomprehensible to an orthodox Jew. He was clearly bewildered by this anomalous use of language and, in an effort to come to grips with its exotic diction, created a palimpsest of erasures, footnotes, exclamation points, and underscores. Questions frame each column of text: "Who is the 'Pellean Conqueror'?"; "Where is the 'City of Gallaphrone'?"; and "Why did Milton write 'deep on his Front engraven / Deliberation sat and public care' when all he meant was 'he frowned'?" Irritated by the pointlessness of the poet's erudition, he tried desperately to jimmy the lock of this baffling work, to find out what was inside, what message it contained, what conceivable purpose these dog-eared pages were intended to serve, and how they could possibly be relevant to the life of a brainy Jewish kid from Chicago's South Side.

My father never answered the questions that his spidery script still poses over fifty years later. Although he earned a Ph.D. in clinical psychology, his life was, after this one brief encounter with poetry, devoid of art and literature. It was not pleasure or curiosity that goaded him to excel in school but a distinctly un-Miltonic muse: his mother. Having lost her husband when my father was eight, she worked as a seamstress who, supporting her family by means of her Singer sewing machine in a tenement slum, bullied her son through college and instilled in him a precept he passed on to his children: that reading and education were a means, never an end; that they were tools of social advancement, of escaping the toils of grinding poverty and entering a higher social class. He did not read—he studied, he acquired credentials, built his résumé, and then, once his career was in full swing, ceased reading altogether, the specter of destitution having been vanquished by a two-car garage and a comfortable split-level on a wooded lot in an affluent neighborhood. During my childhood, as he hustled to support his family while earning his doctorate, he never read in the living room or the kitchen, where we could see and imitate him, but only locked away in his study, where he gladly exchanged one form of drudgery for another: the unpleasant task of raising three loud and ill-mannered children for the tedium of his class work. He shirked his parental responsibilities so completely that Mother often jokingly referred to him not as "your father" but, metonymically, as "the crack of light beneath the backroom door." Ours was, despite all of the books that lined the sagging shelves of his study, a bookless family and mine the education of a typical American philistine. I have no memories of being read to as a child and do not even recall whether there were any books among my toys, reading and playing being two mutually exclusive activities in this joylessly studious family.

Under such circumstances, it is not surprising that I fell in love with books only after a lifetime of abusing and misunderstanding them, of exploiting them to manipulate the world to my advantage, to win the accolades of my teachers and display my superior culture to homophobes, who, even when I was a child, taunted me for holding my books "like a girl," clutched maternally to my breast. When I was young I shared my father's belief that school simply provided a vocational apprenticeship in which one ran neck and neck with other competitors, who must be squeezed out of the market, forced to give way in astonished admiration before one's high test scores and brilliantly written term papers. Books were like vitamin pills and wholesome food: they were "nutritious," "good for me." I did not bother to taste them, I simply shoveled them down.

As an adolescent, I was naïvely obsessed with mastering all knowledge and culture, with becoming a living encyclopedia, a task I undertook with grim conscientiousness and an amazing lack of selectivity. When I began to study the Romantic poets, for instance, I would open Coleridge's *Poetical Works* at page 1 and read straight through, line after line, to page 606, devouring the fragments, juvenilia, first drafts, metrical experiments, and nonsense verse with the same palpable lack of enthusiasm with which I read "Christabel," "Frost at Midnight," and "The Rime of the Ancient Mariner." After I polished off Coleridge, who was no sooner read than forgotten, I would just as dispiritedly plow through the complete Shelley and again read every fragment, hymn, stray stanza, epitaph, dirge, epithalamium, song, and poetic drama, never stopping for a second to consider whether I was enjoying myself (which I most decidedly was not) or whether I made any aesthetic distinction between "Adonais" and the footnotes at the bottom of the page. For years, I kept track of the number of hours I read per day and was full of bitter self-recriminations if I read fewer than nine. I even forced myself to make up every minute I missed on the previous day and drove myself so mercilessly that once, in a fit of self-destructive rage over the dereliction of my literary duties, I took a pair of scissors and chopped off all of my hair. To the dismay of my colleagues at the day care center, I wore my shame to work the next day like the scarlet *L* for Laziness, the badge of humiliation of a puritan crank who read books as anorectics count calories, in a spirit of uncontrollably sadistic self-punishment. I would also obsessively calculate how many books I could cover in the course of a lifetime if I kept reading at my current pace, only to discover that, if I was lucky, I could never possibly exceed a measly 10,000, a pitiful figure that inspired me with gloomy feelings of inadequacy, given the 17,000,000 books in the Library of Congress and the additional 60,000 published every year.

My compulsion to study was so all-consuming that in order to improve my language skills, for a large part of my adolescence I allowed myself to masturbate only when I read the marquis de Sade in French, a perverse testament to my literary extremism, especially since I found de Sade's noxiously written effusions about rape, torture, and dismemberment completely unarousing. To this day, the zealotry of my youth remains alive in what my friends laughingly refer to as my "reeducation project," an ongoing campaign in which I memorize the basic facts of world history by studying high school textbooks while working out on my stationary bicycle or even while going to the bathroom, where I read one page of history per poop. I not only ponder every truism on Celestial Seasonings tea bags but also, on the subway, when I am not memorizing the history of philosophy, another essential course in my reeducation project, read all of the poems so generously posted by various arts councils (including the sensitive multicultural ones, which I detest) and even try to translate into English the advertisements in Spanish, unwilling to lose even a second in my lifelong project of self-improvement.

For much of my education, I have been victimized by a typically American view of culture: the quantifiable view, the idea that knowledge can be contained within a limited number of books, that it has precisely drawn boundaries that have been carefully mapped out and explored, that becoming a well-read person is simply a matter of reading every title on a predetermined list. When I was a child, my father purchased for the family the *World Book Encyclopedia*, perhaps on a layaway plan or even from some door-to-door peddler who sold it to him as a magical device that would guarantee his children instant omniscience. I grew up believing that knowledge occupied actual physical space, that it could be reduced to a cubic meter of printed matter, and that all I needed to do was start at "aardvark" and slog my way through to "zyzzyva" to become an intellectual, if not overnight, then at least within a reasonable period of time.

I still suffer from this quantifiable attitude towards reading. It is enshrined in my collection of Penguin

Classics, which I adore looking at, especially the more uniform, older black editions, which have unfortunately been superseded by volumes of differing heights whose spines are adorned with distracting colored bands and small reproductions of paintings, an unwelcome innovation that I hated when it first appeared and continue to dislike. What attracts me to the old Penguins is the psychological implications of their aesthetic monotony, the comfortable feeling they convey that what I need to know can be found on one shelf in a single series, that culture is not amorphous and incalculable but limited and quite manageable. Like the *World Book Encyclopedia*, my Penguins loudly proclaim the finitude of learning, allowing me to believe that all of mankind's intellectual accomplishments stand neatly shelved in my living room.[1]

My intense anxieties about drowning in a sea of books stem in part from the fact that I am a nouveau intellectual, like a member of the nouveaux riches: a reader who was not to the manor born but a vulgar upstart who

[1] My own adolescent campaign to perform the impossible task of learning everything was, I would argue, motivated by the same fear that leads people not only to establish canons of Great Books but also, in the case of the postmodernists, to demolish these canons. Both humanists and theorists are frightened by the immensity of culture and make desperate measures to keep it from straying from a well-trodden path, particularly the theorists, whose duplicitous efforts to open the canon are in fact thinly disguised attempts to close it, to create an even more manageable reading list by substituting a handful of minority writers for the bewildering multiplicity of the "classics." It is perhaps the pragmatic American can-do philosophy that prevents us from realizing that some tasks are simply beyond our capacity, that we must learn to live with our ignorance, an ignorance made all the more painful by centuries of cultural inferiority to Europe.

achieved his literary station in life by clawing his way to the top. Despite my father's Ph.D., we were a family of barbarians, and my early experiences with books reflected my unfamiliarity with culture, my fear of it as a social trap, a potentially humiliating ordeal in which at any moment I might commit a gross social gaffe, like using the wrong fork or drinking out of the finger bowl.

Nouveaux intellectuals are as uncomfortable with books as chimney sweeps at a debutante ball, terrified that others will unmask them as gate crashers and expose their illiterate pedigree. Our fears of being frauds have been exacerbated by the enormous rifts that have opened up between generations because of the ready availability of public education. The almost ten years I spent in college and graduate school have estranged me profoundly from my family and left me with the odd sense that I am "no one in particular," my own creation, that I am parentless, sui generis, an anomaly that produced itself not through insemination but through education. My paternal great-grandfather was a ragpicker, my maternal grandfather an illiterate sharecropper, and several of my Southern uncles actually participated in a lynching, hiring a white whore to entice a black man into her bed and then stringing him from a tree for raping her. What stands between my white-robed, cross-burning uncles and a sensitive gay liberal living in Brooklyn, teaching himself art history, and spending his leisure time at the Metropolitan Museum is an impenetrable wall of books, a lifetime of printed matter that has accelerated time exponentially, cut me adrift from my genealogical history, and severed links with anyone outside of my immediate family. Education has introduced extraordinary discontinuities between the generations, radical discrepancies of sensibility, differences of outlook even more divisive than those created by wars that pitted father against son. In my world, books are thicker than blood. My real family is not my biological family but a circle of friends united by their passion for reading. My father and mother gave me life; books gave me personality, a second life.

For centuries, fiction has been disparaged as the source of neurotic self-delusions, pipe dreams that cause discontent among Don Quixotes and Emma Bovarys, characters who invented new identities for themselves through the books they read. It is almost a topos that reading too many romantic stories causes maladjustment, a desire to be something one is not and can never be, a view of books that was perhaps appropriate for a world in which there was no social mobility, in which people remained in the station in which they were born, a rut whose tranquillity was disrupted by those who dared to dream of greener pastures, aspiring to rise above the mediocrity of an unacceptable life.

In a world in which mass education has allowed virtually anyone to jump from class to class, reading can no longer be condemned as a cause of dissatisfaction and restlessness but must be celebrated as the vehicle for change, a way of improving oneself, of imagining a different kind of life and then creating it, an alternative unavailable to Emma Bovary, trapped in the provinces with her amorous fantasies. Flanked by ragpickers on one side and grand dragons on the other, I felt suspended in an historical vacuum as a child. I was a tabula rasa waiting to be inscribed with a brand-new story, one that books and education would create for me.

When Jacqueline Susann's *Valley of the Dolls* appeared in 1966, I was one of its most ardent admirers. Although I was only nine, I was so captivated by its decadent world of sex-crazed pill poppers hounded by the paparazzi, drowning their sorrows in money and booze, contacting deadly diseases and turning belly up in their swimming pools, that I set out to write its sequel, a lurid bodice ripper in which I myself starred as a jet-setting playboy paradoxically afflicted—this was the sole biographical truth in my saga—by the fear of flying, a phobia that, at pivotal moments in the narrative, caused humiliating bouts of incontinence. Susann was the first writer to leave her autograph on the blank white page of my personality, offering me a vision of life dramatically different from the one I led in Republican Wisconsin, a land of rugged farmers whose sons, their boots caked with manure, ridiculed unathletic mama's boys like myself. Although the word "fag" appears on virtually every page of *Valley of the Dolls,* I was drawn to this dark vision of a substance-abusing demimonde precisely because it contained so many homosexuals, whereas it seemed unlikely, so far as I could tell, that there were any queens whatsoever hiding out amidst the cow patties of Wisconsin's dairy farms. From the beginning of my life, books were integral to my process of self-invention, of writing a new story on the pages of a record from which my family had erased its own history, one I composed by channeling an eclectic series of authors, from Susann and Abraham Maslow to Thoreau and Proust.

I became a committed reader only at the age of fourteen, when I fell under the spell of the loud, domineering, glamorous, abusive, and charismatic principal of the small alternative high school I attended in the early 1970s. It was the startling enthusiasm with which this emasculating but thrillingly intelligent prima donna read that changed my life forever, and when she died three years ago, I cried to hear that it had happened while she was reading in bed, the book slipping from her hands midsentence. At the Newfound School, which she owned and ran, I fell in love with my history teacher, Greg, a handsome athlete who quickly adopted me as his acolyte and lent me stacks of his own books, which I whipped through at lightning speed in order to win his approval. For two years, I read solely to please him. My unrequited obsession assumed an oddly literary form in which I accepted his offerings as if they were a lover's gifts, tributes I rewarded with my rapt attention and meticulous commentary. Reading was a covert means of seduction, of courtship, of expressing my sexual submission, a vicarious form of lovemaking with a staunchly heterosexual man who lent me books that became embodiments of my inexpressible desires, longings that I kept tactfully wrapped in paper jackets.

Greg's particular interest was pop psychology, and so for two years I immersed myself in the works of Rollo May, Eric Fromm, and Abraham Maslow, authors I would later detest, but that, in the presence of Greg's broad shoulders and massive chest, I found unutterably fascinating, feigning that I was "self-actualizing" as others might feign they were hearing deceased spirits or speaking in tongues. During my stint as a human potentialist, I was the equivalent of the nineteenth-century heroine in du Maurier's melodrama *Trilby* and Greg, the equivalent of the mesmerist Svengali, whom I appeased not by singing opera before the European nobility but by performing a lengthy literary servitude. Other disciples sacrifice small animals to their gods; I sacrificed books, mumbling rubbish about achieving my "interpersonal goals" and striving for excellence, my eyes fixed squarely on Greg's physique.

Greg was no sooner out of sight and out of mind than, for the ultimate good of my sanity, I dropped pop psychology and, entering college, promptly became the creature of another intellectual despot, and then, when this relationship failed, yet another. Their Svengalism was just as tyrannical, literary, and covertly sexual as Greg's. For several years, I performed for their benefit, as an expression of homage to their good looks, a full-time impersonation of a Transcendental priestess, a nature-worshipping Thoreauvian, a milkmaid poetess whose antics still fill me with horror. My frustrated sexual desires for these two heterosexual autocrats were channeled through books, as well as the poems they wrote, which they lent me more or less as scripts for an ecstatic performance that I staged in the long, melancholy walks I took in stormy weather, battered by the elements, my face streaming with rain, my shoulder-length hair tossed by the winds, and that I reenacted in both my readings and my diaries, documents that have forever destroyed any illusion of either the precocity or the innocence of my youth. At the age of eighteen, having been assigned Denise Levertov's *Taste and See* by the first of these new mentors, I wrote:

> Her poetry rings for me, and each word seems as
> if a vital organ in some living whole. There are
> things that I know when I see them. Young as I am,
> I know when a poet has taken hold of the world
> and glimpsed the essence of things. I am so moved.
> I am calmed by her kind words that rise and fall. I
> am strengthened and made whole again. I am deter-
> mined to be a poet whose soul speaks as lightly and
> as profoundly as I have heard her soul speak. . . .
> To read and write poetry, that will make my life
> noble and strong. She has done what a poet must
> do: we have opened each other's souls. I live on her
> great faith in living.

Every book I read was simply an anthropomorphic extension of myself, every poet an intimate friend who was as impressed by the depths of my sagacity as I was by theirs. There was no distinction between my trumped-up inner life and the religious material that my two masters were giving me, which functioned like a gut-wrenching laxative that released a spate of sensitive, milkmaidish poesie:

> *I hear the wind:*
> *it rises and falls,*
> *it speaks and listens,*
> *I hear the wind,*
> *the soul,*
> *and the tongue.*
> *Loudly it speaks,*
> *now softly*
> *and loudly*
> *and gently again.*

> *The winds blow, I feel as if*
> *My soul had been caught like a kite*
> *In a tree, scattered like mist that clings to the branches,*
> *The winds are blowing. I feel as if the wind.*
> *I should be a poet where the words blow*
> *About me like the sounds of birds*
> *Which a feeble arm reaches to hold:*
> *But in my winds there are few words.*

Cumulatively, my poems constitute an unwitting portrait of an adolescent without an identity, "a kite caught in a tree," the perfect candidate for fascist takeovers by the mentors who ambushed me throughout my youth. The very diction of my poems suggests my pathological malleability, willessness, and emotional vacuity: "soft," "sad," "gentle," "feeble," "shifting," and "silent." I am not a creature of flesh and blood but of "shadows," "clouds," and "mists." I do not breath, I "sigh," I "murmur." I do not walk with my feet planted firmly on the ground, I hover over it, I flit, I "rise and fall," rocked like a baby in a cradle, an insubstantial wraith blown hither and yon by melancholy zephyrs. Devoid of judgments, decisions, and opinions, this lifeless apparition, this "feeble arm" clutching at moonbeams, was the perfect protégé for more dominant personalities, who needed my flattery, defining themselves through the idealized reflections cast by my fawning eyes.

At the age of nineteen I fell in love with a different sort of man: a gay man, a milestone in my sexual and intellectual development. While just as unrequited as my obsessions with the three men who preceded Philip, my pathological fixation on this reserved and intelligent person, who was to remain my dearest friend until his murder some fifteen years later, differed from the indentured servitude of my earlier literary affairs in one key respect: we were both openly gay, and although Philip was from the beginning unsparingly candid about his lack of interest in me, he treated me with deep compassion as — to our mutual distress — I slowly stripped myself of every last shred of dignity in my pursuit of him. Before I met Philip, the books my masters commanded me to read contained mysterious intimations of the Love That Dared Not Speak Its Name, but when the Name could at last be spoken, the whole elaborate ritual of passing books back and forth, deliciously sharing secret literary confidences, and making love to my mentors by adoring their favorite authors and deferring to their superior tastes was rendered unnecessary. Never again would I use books as a means of seduction, of achieving intimacy with men oblivious to my designs, playing the role of the false ingenue who longed for something warmer than the cold, cerebral clasp of an intellectual brotherhood.

And yet my relationship with Philip was not entirely free of literature. Early in our friendship, I began to read Proust, whom I adopted as the muse of my new obsession, an author who inspired me to degrade myself as recklessly as Swann degraded himself before Odette. I begged Philip to sleep with me, forced my way into parties to which I was not invited because I was certain that he would meet someone, and constantly nagged him with paranoid accusations about sexual overtures I wrongfully imagined he had made to men. As a child, I projected myself into the works of the queen of pulp fiction, Jacqueline Susann, stepping right into her mod Pucci pantsuits (which Rex Reed once called her "banana-split nightmares"). Now I was projecting myself into the works of an author at the opposite end of the spectrum, a master of modernism at its most inaccessibly highbrow, the narrator of *A la recherche du temps perdu*, whose fixation on Albertine became the model for my own complex feelings for Philip. The book's effect on me was disastrously permissive. It glamorized my obsessive behavior and inadvertently encouraged me to let myself go, to become as fascinatingly wretched as the protagonist of Proust's novel, a crazed lunatic who peeked out of the third-floor window of Oberlin College's library to determine which direction Philip would turn when he descended the ramp after an evening spent studying by my side: to the right — peace of mind, for it meant he was returning to his apartment, alone; to the left — despair, for it suggested a midnight tryst with an unknown stranger at the college bar. I had advanced in my theatrical career, from bit parts as the milkmaid poetess to a starring role as the lovesick inamorato, an Othello tormented by grotesque sexual nightmares. Even in the midst of my indisputably genuine suffering, I was still playacting, still taking my emotional cues from books, which added an element of literary piquancy to my love for Philip.

Self-creation through fiction and poetry ended abruptly when I experienced a devastating loss of faith in the greatness of books, a deconversion that occurred when I began reviewing for gay newspapers in the early 1980s. Having read canonical texts almost exclusively since high school, I was entirely unprepared for the raw sewage into which I was suddenly plunged when I was assigned the novels produced by small gay publishers like Alyson and Gay Men's Press, the house organs of glad-to-be-gay "movement fiction," which churned out seemingly endless numbers of social-realist tracts in the guise of novels. I was so sickened by these books both as propaganda and as physical objects, often adorned with lurid covers of rainbow freedom flags unfurling victoriously in the wind or of glistening Fabios clad in scanty loincloths, that I began to indulge in my own form of book burning. I used a stack of review copies to replace the missing leg of a battered sofa, chose a particularly unsavory volume to prop up a window, and crammed paperbacks into my rotting kitchen wainscoting and entombed them beneath a mound of steel wool soaked in plaster in order to curb an infestation of mice. I had always treated books with the utmost respect, removing their jackets before I read them and opening even the cheapest mass paperbacks cautiously lest I crack their brittle spines, but I now found myself unceremoniously tossing them in the trash and splattering them with coffee grounds, ripping them in two as kindling for fires, and using them as flyswatters to smash mosquitoes on summer nights.

This desanctifying of books was vitally important to me for a number of reasons. I had at last become a practicing literary agnostic and would never again look at books as revered missals to be accepted unquestioningly from the hands of my idols, who were dethroned along with their central tool of mind control, which I had desecrated without being struck by lightning, blasphemed and lived to tell about it. My new critical attitude towards reading precluded the very possibility of hero worship, which had grown out of my belief in the holiness of books, a superstitious gullibility shaken to its foundations by this unforeseen collision with the mediocre and the maladroit. Moreover, on purely literary grounds, reading bad books dramatically enhanced the pleasure of good ones. I had lived in a rarefied intellectual atmosphere in which every author was "great," a "classic," and had therefore become like a spoiled rich kid inured to his own wealth, so accustomed to his good fortune that he had no standard of comparison to assess the extent of his prosperity, no way of knowing that real artistic culture did not consist solely of masterpieces that flowered in a vacuum like gorgeous hothouse orchids but of a compost heap of dreck in which good books were firmly rooted, poking their heads out of a reeking mountain of fertilizing shit. I suddenly realized the necessity of acquiring taste to negotiate the perilous passages of a world that was not as safely and monotonously "excellent" as I had been taught to believe. With the birth of my critical faculties came a new invulnerability to the literary decrees of my mentors. Acquiring taste meant acquiring independence, which went hand in hand with acquiring personality, a fully formed identity that could not simply be evacuated with each new god I doted on, the slate wiped clean to receive a brand-new set of literary instructions, the human potentialists giving way in the blink of an eye to the Transcendentalists.

During my lengthy apprenticeship to my masters, reading was a private activity that took place alone in my room only to be shared during tête-à-têtes where I showed off my obedience and hard work. Now that I had achieved my intellectual majority, I began to read in public, a further desanctifying of literature, which I now studied in cafés and cafeterias, my books spread out next to overflowing ashtrays, dirty coffee cups, and plates heaped with unappetizing scoops of shepherd's pie, no longer the sacraments of a religion of hero worship but the pedestrian tools of the scholarly trade I was learning. And yet up until this point reading had been about love, about finding my Platonic soul mate, the missing half that I now sought in public places, bearing a placard that would identify myself to him, unmistakable signs that read *The Eustace Diamonds, Mimesis, The Anatomy of Melancholy,* and *European Literature and the Latin Middle Ages.* Desperate to establish contact with other intellectuals, I became an obscene literary exhibitionist who flashed the covers of his books at perfect strangers, hoping that such signals would be intercepted by like-minded readers stranded in distant galaxies.

The search for signs of intelligent life in the universe was, however, a lonely and futile one, as became particularly apparent when I moved to San Francisco, where I read nightly at the Café Flore, a hangout that doubled as a coffee shop and a high-fashion catwalk for gay poseurs. Once while writing an essay on the language used by New Age channelers, I found myself in the uncharacteristically shamefaced position of wanting to conceal the titles of the paperbacks I was reading, which I achieved by taping together plain white jackets on which I facetiously printed the titles *Pride and Prejudice* and *War and Peace,* thus hiding the toothsome grins of such workshop facilitators as Jack Persel and J. Z. Knight. I could not bear the thought that anyone would think that I was reading the wisdom of Ramtha[©] and Lazaris for my own edification, even though the very few people who actually did read in the Flore sat, more often than not, with their noses buried in the pages of *The Celestine Prophecy, Understanding Your Angels and Meeting Your Spirit Guides,* and *Igniting Your Soul Life.* The truth is that had I been perusing *Mein Kampf* no one would have noticed, for I was playing to a nonexistent gallery, the empty hall before which the intellectual persists in strutting so pointlessly, brandishing his esoteric titles for the benefit of an extinct tribe of book lovers. The heartbreaking sadness of this game of literary exhibitionism also emerges in the pride I still feel when tricks stand awestruck in front of my library and say, with genuine amazement, "All these books!"—a perfunctory tribute to the life of the mind that only testifies to its complete irrelevance to them. Once while giving a telephone repairman a blow job, I was thrilled as, in the very middle of the act, I noticed his eyes roaming in admiration over the titles on my shelves, passing from my Penguins to my dictionaries to my art books, a response even more exciting than the moans he uttered in reaction to my vigorous attentions.

My public exile as a wandering reader who migrated from coffee shop to coffee shop seeking his soul mates was closely related to the act of cruising for sex. I would often kill two birds with one stone and pursue my studies of seventeenth-century prose style while ogling the parade of young men milling about me, my eyes darting back and forth between Jeremy Taylor's *The Rule and Exercises of Holy Dying* and the svelte bodies and handsome faces of virile young Bostonians. Friends often affectionately mocked my distinctive style of reading, which they characterized as a palsied nodding up and down, as if my attention were split between two screens, two equally magnetic attractions, the words on the page and the boys in the band.

And yet as eagerly as I cast lascivious glances at men, I jealously protected my privacy and loathed being disturbed by other coffee shop habitués who viewed my daily presence in the café as an open invitation to sit down and shoot the breeze while I remained in a state of enraged paralysis, my face a mask of inhospitable disapproval, my eyes drawn irresistibly back to the book I longed to immerse myself in. Among my closest friends, my stand-offishness during these unwelcome intrusions was known as "dropping the glass curtain," an invisible barrier of reserve that came crashing down the instant anyone presumed to encroach on my territory and steal from me precious time intended for my work. The dilemma of reading in public became a metaphor for my entire life, for the communal misanthropy of an isolated intellectual who at once enjoyed the pleasures of being in public and yet kept the public at arm's length, mingled with his own kind and yet remained in a state of privacy, occupying a no-man's-land that served as a compromise between the loneliness of the study and the annoying distractions of the crowd. Books were my one-way mirror, a magical cloak of invisibility that allowed me, at least in my imagination, to pretend that though I could see others, I myself could not be seen, that I was a spy, an observer who enjoyed a highly mediated contact with the world, my eyes peeping over the spines of *Areopagitica* and *The Anniversaries*. Books gave me both a vantage point on the world and a safe refuge from it, a retreat to which I fled, ducking behind covers in a game of hide-and-seek the moment that someone caught me, meddlesome busybody that I was, rudely gaping at them.

My dislike of the public and my animal need to establish some kind of superficial contact with my kind can also be seen in the intense separation anxiety I experience on the very few occasions I venture out of doors without a book. There is little practical reason for carrying as many volumes as I do in my book bag for the forty-five-minute commute to the Metropolitan or to my doctor's office in Soho, for even if the subway should sit parked on the tracks for hours, I can seldom concentrate enough to read but waste my time instead sighing in irritated disgust. When I lived in Boston, one of the other habitués at my favorite coffee shop used to stack around him a wall of books, pulling out of his seemingly bottomless backpack some fifteen or twenty, which remained untouched for the duration of his stay, serving only as a safe enclosure in which he flagrantly picked his nose as he thumbed the pages of a novel. Recently, in the middle of the night, I experienced a rare panic attack in which, as is often the case with this alarming syndrome, I became convinced that I was dying. I left the house with four things: my clothing, my keys, my wallet, and a book, *Swann's Way*, an inappropriate novel—to say the least—for a busy inner-city emergency room, where Proust's labyrinthine sentences and somewhat precious observations swam before my eyes as the old black woman on one side of my gurney sank into a stertorous coma and the man on the other shrieked like a victim of the Inquisition as his doctors struggled to reset the bones of his broken leg.

In part, I need to carry a book on my person at all times because I need to identify myself to others as an intellectual, much as doctors wear their stethoscopes and policemen their badges. But I also cling to my novel for exactly the same reason women cling to their purses, as a security blanket that calms the fear of being in public and provides a symbolic reminder of home life and privacy, the domestic comforts squirreled away in messy caches of lip balms, hand lotions, used tissues, and throat lozenges. Likewise, books are for me the ultimate symbol of privacy and are therefore essential provisions for my forays into a foreign world, where I carry with me a token of the peace I find night after night stretched out in my red recliner.

My separation anxiety from books has been a major fear of mine since adolescence, when I began to suffer from a recurrent nightmare, that I would one day be stranded in the hinterlands without access to a public library, an obsession that led me to amass books much as Mormons stockpile provisions in their pantries, convinced that the seventh seal is about to be broken and the Four Horsemen of the Apocalypse to gallop forth across the countryside spreading disease and famine. In my late teens, an encounter with a sinister librarian taught me that my separation anxiety was not as unreal as one might think. Since my father taught part-time in the psychology department at the University of North Carolina at Asheville, his children were entitled to borrowing privileges at the main library, whose collection of books simply gathered dust on the shelves, untouched by the undergraduates, who were too busy winning glory out on the basketball court and the soccer field to read. I took advantage of this underused facility and began studying dozens of books in Spanish, French, and German, all of them with their own manila cards, which in the days before automation needed to be filed alphabetically in a checkout tray that was almost invariably empty, given how few students ever so much as set foot in the building. My nemesis was a stickler for rules who resented filing my cards and, moreover, disliked me for reading so ambitiously. Over a period of months, she imposed more and more restrictions on my privileges, until one day she emerged triumphantly from the sorting room with an officious smirk on her face and announced that my card was no longer valid, that I had "overused" her underused — indeed, *never*-used — library. After reasoning with her and getting nowhere, I lost my temper, called her every name in the book, and then took my case to the dean of students, who was just as unsympathetic, asking me what credentials I could show to justify my using the library as heavily as I did, what degrees I had earned, what university affiliations I could claim — questions that were, without his knowledge, painfully ironic, since it was his son, my

- 231 -

first mentor, the beautiful Greg, who had initially encouraged me to read, while his father was now standing in my way. I stormed out of his office only to be informed, when I returned home, that the dean had called my father to tell him that I was mentally unbalanced and needed immediate psychological help, advice that my father, to his credit and my eternal gratitude, greeted with shouts of anger, asking how the desire to read could possibly be, for an educator like the dean, a sign of emotional instability. Within weeks, with my supply cut off at its source, I left Asheville and moved to Chapel Hill, where the university offered much more liberal lending policies to the members of the community.

Certainly this disgraceful incident contributed to my fear that I would one day find myself library-less. Even now, when I am seized, as I so often am, by fears of destitution and begin to dwell upon the idea that the bottom might fall out of my economy and I would have to leave my relatively spacious apartment and squeeze into a cramped room in a communal house, my first thought is "What in the world would I do with my library?" The truth is that, although I do consult my books frequently, I could easily live without them save for the fact that, as my oldest possessions, they have been incorporated into my very sense of self, into the way I make my world less alienating, less hostile, a familiar place in which I feel safe from the elements. When I imagine a world in which I have failed, in which I am at the end of my rope, abandoned by my friends and family, unable to take care of myself, shivering

- 232 -

in a refrigerator box beneath a bridge, it is always the absence of books that frightens me most, not the absence of food or shelter, but of my beloved library that records what I have made of my life and how I arrived here.

Books helped my father get out of the ghetto and achieve his dreams—a suburban split-level and a time-share in Florida—but they have brought *me* within a stone's throw of shaking a tin can in a subway car, as I have failed monumentally to create the prosperity that my father and grandmother assumed was the inevitable outcome of learning. Because I have refused to work more than two days a week for the last fifteen years, I have deliberately reversed the family fortunes. My grandmother could not have foreseen that I would fall in love with the act of reading as an end in itself, a perverse mania that has led to my financial downfall, to a life in which I have sacrificed my material well-being to my pressing need for unlimited leisure time. Books have become my addictive drug, my heroin, and I have abandoned everything to support my habit. Only the second generation of readers in a family has the luxury of regarding books in an aesthetic and impractical way, the first generation seldom having the confidence to view them as anything other than a means of self-aggrandizement, a view of reading that, in most instances, precludes literary pleasure, which is lost in careerist anxieties about grade point averages and college entrance exams.

Now after thirty years of intensive study, I read alone in my room exclusively for pleasure, not for social gain.

The motivations that led me to acquire culture were entirely illegitimate: to please teachers, to seduce men, to beat competitors, and to achieve intellectual power in the face of humiliating deficiencies in my athletic prowess. And yet despite the self-serving factors that contributed to my intellectual development, the fact remains that, through sheer mechanical repetition, I am now wholly dependent on books and view them not as instruments in a self-promoting scheme but as beautiful objects in their own right. On the threshold of middle age, I am regressing, not maturing, and have embraced the notion that reading is pure play, as fundamentally useless as the activities of a child dabbling in the mud. Perhaps one day I will adopt the same attitude towards my writing, give up my frustrating attempts to secure a readership, ambitions that have only eroded my autonomy and compromised my solitude, and sit down at my desk much as I stretch out in my recliner: in order to enjoy an act that liberates me from the prison of selfhood, one that consumes all of my powers of concentration, that in its intellectual and sensual intensity distracts me from the aggravations of my life.

I began this chapter with an image of my father's *Paradise Lost*, an emblem of the book as a tool, however unserviceable, to advance a poor man's career. I end it with another image, that of my lover's vast library containing books on every conceivable aspect of ancient art, from Greek intaglios and Etruscan mirrors to Sassanian stamp seals and Athenian fictile revetments. Although it seems scarcely possible, John is poorer than I am. He often teeters on the brink of bankruptcy, partly because he suffers from the spendthrift compulsions of a mad bibliophile and, even when money is scarce, thinks nothing of dropping two hundred dollars for a book about Egyptian furniture or red vase painting, which night after night he pores over in his squalid apartment. It is the captivating image of him reading that I have fixed firmly in my mind as the epitome of the disinterested joy in books, so unlike the mirthless rigor with which I flogged myself through the complete poems of the Romantics. No driving ambition is present when he loses himself in the pages of a book, oblivious as he is to the Jamaican music blaring from a window across the way, the Puerto Ricans next door screaming at the top of their lungs, and the rats in the alley squealing in ecstasy as they scrabble through the trash.

12

Ending

As described by many composition instructors, the memoir is actually not a separate genre in its own right but self-help literature in disguise whose primary purpose is "to offer hope and courage to others," to allow authors "to share a little wisdom with their descendants," and to provide their great-great-grandchildren with "a spiritual lift" in their future hour of need. In *How to Write Your Own Life Story*, Lois Daniel concentrates on memoirists who "inspire" their readers with their heroic efforts to overcome insurmountable obstacles, as in the case of a man who, after losing his vision at the age of seventy-two, learns to touch-type so he can continue to write letters to his children, or a paraplegic who masters her depression to become the leader of a national prayer circle. At the core of most memoirs is a Dale Carnegie success story, a rags-to-riches parable that celebrates indomitable human courage, *The Unsinkable Spirit*, to use the title of one recent memoir. In *The Little Red Writing Book,* Lonnie Burnstein Hewitt recommends that, as a way of "breaking into your memory bank," you imagine that you are an animal and then explain why you chose that particular species, an exercise that leads one painfully reserved student to explain that she is as quiet, persevering, and invincible as a turtle and that she hopes to inspire others with "TUR-TLE SPIRIT! TURTLE POWER!"

I do not wish to foster in others TURTLE SPIRIT! TURTLE POWER!, however invigorating I imagine such spunkiness must be. There is nothing inspirational about my life story, nothing that I could confidently ask my readers to emulate. A comment comes to mind that I have always admired by the silent movie actress Louise Brooks, a recluse and alcoholic, who, when questioned by a *Life* magazine reporter writing about retired actresses and their secrets for remaining young and active, avoided the wise clichés of a radiant Ginger Rogers and a gracious Loretta Young and snapped back something to the effect of "no one needs *me* to tell them how to wreck a life."

I am too young to have wrecked my life, and yet what I have written here is not a success story, but a failure story of sorts, a discovery of my own limits, of fatalities, necessities, not my strengths, not my virtues, not my courage in trying times. My father was a pop psychologist and I became a "pop" child, someone who took the hedonistic ideology of consumerism at face value and believed he could be anything he wanted to be and could shape himself into whatever form he chose. In many respects, this is precisely what I have done, creating the personality of no one in particular by rejecting my past, imitating books, and modeling myself on my mentors.

At the age of forty-three, however, I realize that my conviction that I was in charge of my destiny, that my choices were unlimited, was misguided. I am as subject to the vicissitudes of fortune as those who lived before penicillin and the smallpox vaccine. Technological breakthroughs and scientific discoveries made during the Industrial Revolution engendered a false belief in our omnipotence, but I have discovered that many things are beyond my control and have retreated into a somewhat tragic view of life. An epidemic as frightening to those most at risk as the bubonic plague has decimated my generation. My best friend was murdered in Algeria while reporting on the Gulf War. I have not achieved what I set out to achieve as a writer. Even as I finish this book, the relationship that gave me the strength to write it has been called into question in a way I never believed possible. The darling of consumer optimism has discovered the limits of self-creation. My faith in the unfettered human will has come smack against a wall that has risen up before it, an obstruction created by forces I have spent my entire life denying: necessity, accident, and destiny.